# Evangelizing Catholics

## A Mission Manual for the New Evangelization

### Scott Hahn

Our Sunday Visitor Publishing Division
Our Sunday Visitor, Inc.
Huntington, Indiana

*To Pope Francis*

# TABLE OF CONTENTS

# PART I

~

# THE CALL:
# UNDERSTANDING THE
# NEW EVANGELIZATION

# *Chapter 1*

~

# THE NEW EVANGELIZATION:
# A BIRD'S-EYE VIEW

WHAT IS THE NEW EVANGELIZATION?

In some ways, that's a question more easily answered by showing rather than telling. We understand it when we encounter it. We know it when we see it. And over the past few years, I've seen it, up close and personal, in the lives of three of my friends.

Here are their stories.

## A CONVERSION

The year: 2009. The place: The Planned Parenthood abortion facility in Bryan, Texas.

Every morning, as the facility's director, Abby Johnson, left her car and walked toward her office, one of several young pro-life sidewalk counselors would call out to her.

None of the counselors harassed Johnson. They didn't insult her. Whoever was there that day would simply say "Hello," ask Johnson how she was doing, and talk to her about her day. Over time, friendships began to blossom — which meant that when Johnson decided to escape the abortion business that October, she had friends to whom she could turn.[1]

Over the next two years, through her friendships with those sidewalk counselors and other Catholics at the Brazos Valley Coalition for Life, the Baptist-turned-Episcopalian made the decision to enter the Catholic Church.

Johnson received the Eucharist for the first time in December 2011.

## AN AWAKENING

A second story. This one took place in 2004, on Good Friday.

That spring, actor Kevin James was in New York City filming the move *Hitch* with Will Smith. Although James, who was raised Catholic, hadn't officially left the Church, he wasn't practicing the faith either. God and the Mass weren't priorities, and his knowledge of what the Church taught, like that of many Catholics his age, was minimal.

On Good Friday, however, his dad called. During the conversation, James Sr. reminded his son that on that day in particular he needed to tone down the partying and remember what Christ had done for him. As they talked, James walked by a movie theater showing Mel Gibson's *The Passion of the Christ*. He asked his father if it would be appropriate to see that movie on Good Friday. The response? "Absolutely."

Eight years later, in an interview with Raymond Arroyo, James described what happened over the next three hours as "life-changing."

"It completely blew me away," he explained, noting how that movie started him on the path to getting back to Mass, learning more about his faith, and becoming the devout practicing Catholic he is today.[2]

## A HOMECOMING

One final story — one that begins in 1960.

That year, the Beckwith family of New York City welcomed their son, Francis, into the world. Soon after, the family moved to Nevada, and when the time came for the young Beckwith to begin kindergarten, his parents enrolled him in St. Viator's Catholic Elementary School, trusting, as their parents before them did, that the teachers there would instill in their son the fundamentals of the Catholic faith.

Beckwith's religious education began, however, just as the Second Vatican Council came to an end, and continued throughout the tumultuous 1970s. Inside the Church, it was a time of liturgical experimentation and catechetical confusion. Outside the Church, it was a time of moral upheaval and social revolution. The latter problem only exacerbated the former problem, and not until Beckwith stumbled upon the books of Norman Geisler, R. C. Sproul, and Francis Schaeffer did he find the systematic presentation of truth he needed to help him make sense of the world.

Unfortunately, what he found also led him away from the Catholic Church and into evangelical Protestantism.

Decades passed. Beckwith earned his Ph.D. in philosophy and began an illustrious scholarly career, finally settling down as a professor of Church-State Relations at Baylor, the world's largest Baptist University.

In 2006, his reputation as one of evangelical Christianity's most serious thinkers got him elected president of the Evangelical Theological Society. Around the same time, Beckwith's enduring respect for the Church of his childhood began to grow. Attracted to the work of John Paul II, he presented a paper on the pope's contributions to philosophy at a Boston University conference. Afterward, one of the scholars in attendance came up to him with a simple question: "Why aren't you Catholic?"

Beckwith didn't have an answer. So he spent the next year trying to find one — reading the earlier writings of John Paul II's successor, Joseph Ratzinger; hashing out doctrines that he perceived as stumbling blocks to his return to the Church; and talking the question over with his wife and friends. He also devoted long hours to reading the Church Fathers. But it wasn't until his Catholic nephew called and asked Beckwith to be his Confirmation sponsor that the moment of reckoning came. Beckwith knew he had to make a decision, and at long last he knew what that decision needed to be.

Beckwith stepped down from his position as head of the Evangelical Theological Society in May 2007, and he returned to the Catholic Church.[3]

## A CALL

Together, these three snapshots of conversion and reversion give us a composite of the New Evangelization.

In the lives of Abby Johnson, Kevin James, and Francis Beckwith, we see that unlike evangelization in centuries past, the New Evangelization isn't just about shipping off missionaries to foreign shores or sending out mendicant preachers to proclaim the Gospel to pagans. Nor is it evangelization strictly in the sense that many Protestants conceive of evangelization — sharing the Good News with an unbeliever, getting him to confess his faith in Christ, and then moving on to the next unbeliever.

Rather, the New Evangelization is the work of the whole Church — lay, ordained, and consecrated. It's about friends, family, and co-workers reaching out to one another and proclaiming the truth of Christ using all available means — conversation, personal witness, media, and the vast array of intellectual and spiritual riches the Church has built up in her two-thousand-year history. It's about simple acts of kindness, simple challenges issued in love, and simple questions asked with sincerity.

More fundamentally, the New Evangelization is more for the baptized than the unbaptized. It's for those who've been inadequately catechized but all too adequately secularized, and it's for those who've been de-Christianized in the very process of being sacramentalized.

And make no mistake, there are more than a few of those Catholics.

## A Crisis

A few years back, when Pew researchers examined the religious beliefs and presuppositions of Christians in America, they discovered that only 48 percent of Catholics believed beyond a doubt that God was a personal God, a God whom they could know and with whom they could build a relationship. Or, to put it another way, their research showed that 52 percent of Catholics think of God, at least to some degree, as an impersonal force.[4]

It's easy to dismiss those numbers, to argue that those are the Catholics not coming to Church at all or just showing up on Christmas and Easter. But as Sherry Weddell of the

Catherine of Siena Institute points out in her book *Forming Intentional Disciples*, that's simply not the case.

Over the course of thousands of interviews with parish and diocesan leaders, Weddell again and again encountered Catholics who went to Mass every Sunday, who sat on countless committees and served in countless ways, but who nevertheless were skeptical about whether a personal relationship with God was possible.

Moreover, when she asked priests and catechetical leaders from over sixty dioceses around the English-speaking world how many of their parishioners were "intentional disciples" — committed followers of Christ seeking holiness through his Church — the answer she most often received was 5 percent. Again, that's 5 percent of the people who actually come to Church, not simply the baptized at large.[5]

That's the reality of where the Church in the United States (and much of the Western world) is today. That's also why the New Evangelization must go beyond a straightforward proclamation of Gospel basics, instead calling the faithful and unfaithful alike not merely to belief in Christ, but to life in Christ, to a conversion of head and heart that only grows deeper and more profound with each passing year.

The New Evangelization, ultimately, must be a call to every man, woman, and child to fall in love, grow in love, and walk in love with the God who loves us.

Understanding all that matters — not just on an academic level, but also on a practical level. It matters because the New Evangelization is the task to which Christ, through his Church, calls each and every one of us. It is the great work of the Church in the twenty-first century. It is the mission with which you and I have been charged. And it is a mission shot through with the weight of eternity, one for which each of us "will give account to him who is ready to judge the living and the dead" (1 Pet 4:5).

The purpose of this book is to flesh out that mission — what it is, how we carry it out, and what it calls us to proclaim. Think of it as a handbook for the New Evangelization. Or better yet, a mission manual, a guide to help you understand and live what it means to be an evangelized Catholic, as well as an evangelizing Catholic.

So how do we begin that mission?

# Chapter 2
~

# THE NEW EVANGELIZATION:
# A COMMON VISION

WHEN YOU'VE BEEN AROUND for two thousand years, you don't get many "firsts." Most of what you have to say or do has been said or done before. But *Lumen Fidei* ("The Light of Faith") was indeed a first. It was the first encyclical in the history of the Catholic Church written by two popes. Pope Benedict XVI began it. Pope Francis completed it.

In that, it has a singular importance. Unlike any other encyclical, *Lumen Fidei* has the weight of two Successors of Peter behind it. It also is the fruit of the thought and prayers of the two great evangelizers of the twenty-first century, two men who, in a way, are a little like the two great evangelizers of the first century: Peter and Paul, the fisherman and the scholar.

From these two men, and the encyclical they wrote, come our marching orders for the New Evangelization. That is, in effect, what *Lumen Fidei* is: a directive or a blueprint for the mission that lies ahead.

It's not, however, a blueprint for which they alone are responsible. Rather, it's a work to which every pope for the last fifty years has contributed, with its origins reaching back to the Second Vatican Council and beyond.

## THE SEEDS OF THE NEW EVANGELIZATION

In the first part of the twentieth century, long before any pope called the faithful to the work of the New Evangelization, Catholic priests and theologians sought to revitalize the Church's liturgical, devotional, and intellectual life through various renewal movements. These movements then intersected in the 1950s, in what came to be known as the Kerygmatic Movement.

Led by Josef Jungmann and Johannes Hofinger, but also including Jean Cardinal Daniélou, Henri de Lubac, and Hans Urs von Balthasar, the Kerygmatic Movement challenged clergy and laity alike to recover the New Testament *kerygma* — that is, to make the Gospel more central in Catholic preaching, teaching, and life.

So, instead of priests just offering homilies that catechized the faithful on the moral law or the saints, the Kerygmatic theologians wanted to see priests open up the Scriptures, bringing the baptized to a more intimate encounter with Christ through the breaking open of the Word. They also wanted to see Catholics living in a more profound imitation of what they encountered in the Gospels, approaching the life of faith with a newness and freshness reminiscent of the first Christians.

In contrast to many who came before them, Jungmann, Hofinger, and their like saw evangelization not as something merely for those who had never heard the Gospel before but also as an ongoing process, a deepening of faith that unfolded year after year. They likewise believed that the best way to realize that vision of evangelization was by integrating the fruits of the other renewal movements — the Liturgical Renewal, the Biblical Renewal, and the Patristic Renewal — and applying them to both homilies and catechesis.

When the Second Vatican Council convened in 1962, many of the Council Fathers sympathized with the Kerygmatic Movement's goals and built on their theology, incorporating even the movement's evangelical terminology into the council documents.

For example, while in the documents of the First Vatican Council the term "gospel" (*evangelion*) was used just once and then only to refer to one of the four Gospels, a century later, in the documents of Vatican II, you find the word "gospel" mentioned 157 times. Similarly, although Vatican I never referenced the words for "evangelize," "evangelizing," or "evangelization," at Vatican II the verb "evangelize" was used 18 times and the word "evangelization" 31 times.

That unprecedented profusion of terms that refer to the *evangel* and evangelization didn't just signify a change in language. It signified a change in focus, a change that became even more evident through the actions of Pope Paul VI as the council drew to a close.

## TAKING ROOT

If the seeds of the New Evangelization were planted by the Kerygmatic Movement and the Second Vatican Council, then they were watered by the evangelical fervor of Paul VI.

Taking his cue from Vatican II and from his papal namesake, St. Paul, Pope Paul VI picked up this theme of evangelization and ran with it — almost literally — becoming the first pope in history to make apostolic journeys to other continents. He saw himself not just as a prince of the Church or an administrator of the Curia but also as the Church's primary preacher and teacher — in effect, as its "Missionary in Chief."

As such, he was determined to preach the Gospel, in person, in all four corners of the world.

And he did.

In between sessions of Vatican II, in 1964, Paul VI traveled to the Holy Land and then on to India. In 1965, he came to New York City and spoke at the United Nations. Two years later, he headed off to Portugal and the Muslim-dominated country of Turkey. In 1968, he visited Columbia; in 1969, he went to Uganda; and in 1970, a record-breaking year, he flew to Iran, East Pakistan, the Philippines, West Samoa, Australia, Indonesia, Hong Kong, and Sri Lanka. By the end of Paul VI's papacy, there was no continent on which Peter hadn't preached.

The pope's passion for evangelization, however, went beyond his travels. Two years after the final session of Vatican II, he reorganized the Roman Curia, changing the name for the Congregation of the Propagation of the Faith to the Congregation for the Evangelization of Peoples. Then, in 1974, he penned the apostolic exhortation *Evangelii Nuntiandi* — in English, "On Evangelization in the Modern World."

There, he made it clear that all this emphasis on evangelization was not just a passing fad in a post-conciliar Church.

Evangelization, he wrote, "is in fact the grace and vocation most proper to the Church, her deepest identity. She exists in order to evangelize ... to be the channel of the gift of grace, to reconcile sinners with God, and to perpetuate Christ's sacrifice in the Mass, which is the memorial of His death and glorious Resurrection" (n. 14).


## FIRST SHOOTS


Building on the Kerygmatic Movement, the Second Vatican Council, and the papacy of Paul VI, Pope John Paul II quietly launched the New Evangelization in a field in Poland on a June day in 1979.

While speaking in Nowa Hutta — a town constructed by the communists as the "ideal" workers town, but which, in reality, was anything but — John Paul II called for a new evangelization for the new millennium. Few people, however, took note of the call. Fewer still understood it.

In part, that's because the pope didn't go into detail about what he meant by a "new evangelization." It was just one line in one speech. Moreover, the fact of the address overshadowed the lone line. It occurred during John Paul II's first visit to his homeland following his election to the papacy, which meant the spotlight was on him and how the communist authorities responded to his words, more than the actual words.

Four years later, however, during an address to the Latin American bishops' conference in Port-au-Prince, Haiti, John Paul II issued the call again. This time the world noticed.

To the bishops gathered there, he explained, "The commemoration of the half millennium of evangelization will gain its full energy if it is a commitment not to re-evangelize, but to a New Evangelization, new in its ardor, methods, and expression."[6]

In that explanation, the pope pointed ahead to 1992, the year that would mark the five hundredth anniversary of the founding and first evangelization of the Americas. He also, in a way, entrusted the primary work of the New Evangelization to Catholics in the Americas, in effect asking us to take it on as our own particular task.

The entrusting was fitting. After all, five hundred years before, when the evangelization of the Americas began, the most populous Catholic countries in the world were in Europe: Italy, Spain, and France. By 1983, that was no longer the case. The faith had all but collapsed in Europe, and the most populous Catholic countries in the world, then as now, were

Brazil, Mexico, and the United States, countries that hadn't even existed five centuries earlier. A seismic shift had taken place, and John Paul II saw the hand of God in that. He believed that the countries born in the wake of that earlier evangelization had a unique role to play in this new evangelization, a role made all the more urgent in light of the fate of the Faith in Europe.

Where will Catholics in the Americas find themselves in five hundred years if Catholics today don't take up the call of the New Evangelization? That's the question he wanted us to ask ourselves.

In pointing forward to 1992, however, John Paul II wasn't just referencing Christopher Columbus and the old evangelization. He also was making it clear that the New Evangelization was not a project that would be over and done in a day. The first evangelization of the Americas took decades, centuries really, to take root, and this new evangelization was to be no different.

The pope made that even clearer in *Redemptoris Missio*, where he explained that he envisioned the 1990s as an "Advent season" of the New Evangelization, with the real work to commence in the new millennium.[7] By that, he meant that just as the four weeks leading up to Christmas are a time of preparation before the celebration of Christ's birth, the 1990s were to be a time of preparation, a time for readying the soil necessary for the New Evangelization to come into full flower.

## FERTILIZATION

Throughout the decade leading up to the new millennium, John Paul II made ready for the New Evangelization in countless ways — through encyclicals and synods, apostolic exhortations and general audiences, papal travels and long hours of prayer. In 1992, he promulgated the first universal *Catechism of the Catholic Church* in four hundred years, a catechism which has served as one of the primary instruments of evangelization. Then, a year later, he traveled to Denver, Colorado, for the sixth World Youth Day.

John Paul II himself chose the location for the event, telling James Cardinal Stafford, then archbishop of the city, that he had become convinced through prayer that the next World Youth Day must take place in Denver.[8]

Many within the Church, however, disagreed. To them, the decision seemed ill fated. Previous World Youth Days had taken place in cities and countries with large Catholic populations and age-old traditions of Catholic pilgrimage: Rome, Santiago de Compostela, Buenos Aires, and Czestochowa. No such tradition existed in the American Rockies. So the critics predicted failure. American young people were too sophisticated to be interested in this Polish pope, they warned.

But the crowds of young people thronging Denver's Mile High Stadium and surrounding grounds — crowds that eventually grew to more than half a million — proved those critics wrong. As the reporters crumpled up their pre-written stories about the day's failure, the pope made it clear to the young people gathered there that the New Evangelization was their special task, a mission entrusted in a singular way to their generation.

"Each one of you must have the courage to go and spread the Good News among young people your own age who will then take the Church and society into the next century," he said.[9]

Looking back, that day in many ways was *the* turning point for the New Evangelization in America. From it, hundreds if not thousands of initiatives at the parish and diocesan level sprang up, while countless numbers of the young people in attendance have since gone on to dedicate their lives to teaching the faith and serving the Church, as well as inspiring others to do the same.

Denver, of course, was just one moment of many in the "Advent season" of the New Evangelization. Throughout the 1990s, John Paul II returned again and again to the idea, building on what he wrote in his encyclical *Redemptoris Missio*: "I sense that the moment has come to commit all of the Church's energies to a new evangelization.... No believer in Christ, no institution of the Church can avoid this supreme duty: to proclaim Christ to all peoples" (n. 3).

One more time: "No believer in Christ, no institution of the Church can avoid this supreme duty." That is to say, when it comes to evangelization, there are no exceptions. There are no exemptions. Nor is there any duty more paramount.

If you're looking for your marching orders, look no further.

## A GROWING SEASON

That duty — to proclaim Christ to all peoples — didn't end with John Paul II's death. Nor did papal calls for the faithful to carry out that duty cease. If anything, they grew more urgent.

Throughout his papacy, again and again, Pope Benedict emphasized the need for both primary evangelization (sharing the Gospel with those who have never heard of Christ) and secondary evangelization (a sort of re-evangelization in places that have lost a living sense of the faith).

Less than a year after his succession to the Chair of Peter, Benedict marked the fortieth anniversary of Vatican II's *Ad Gentes* (on the missionary activity of the Church) by noting that, "[Evangelization] is not an option but the vocation proper to the People of God, a duty incumbent upon it by the command of the Lord Jesus Christ himself (cf. *Evangelii Nuntiandi*)."[10]

A year later, at the Vatican, he said he hoped that "through prayer, witness of life, and Christian commitment in all its forms … every member of the faithful may be a missionary where she or he lives. I also hope for the birth of vocations to proclaim the Gospel to people who do not yet know it."[11]

Yet again, at the 2009 World Youth Day, the pope declared, "The main task for us all is that of a new evangelization aimed at helping younger generations to rediscover the true face of God, who is Love."[12]

Benedict also explained in 2009 that carrying out that work was the primary task of his papacy, writing, "Leading men and women to God, to the God who speaks in the Bible: this is the supreme and fundamental priority of the Church and of the Successor of Peter at the present time."[13]

As the years passed, Pope Benedict's focus on the New Evangelization only grew more intense, culminating, in a way, in 2011.

In February of that year, Pope Benedict XVI announced that the 13th General Assembly of the Synod of Bishops would take place in October 2012. He also announced the theme of the bishops' discussion: "The New Evangelization for the Transmission of the Christian Faith."

Four months later, on the feast of Sts. Peter and Paul, Benedict had another announcement. This time, he shared his plan for the formation of a new dicastery in the Roman Curia, the Pontifical Council for Promoting the New Evangelization. Finally, in the fall of 2011, he called for a Year of Faith to begin the following October, a Year of Faith that would serve as a sort of spiritual boot camp to help the Church better prepare for the work of the New Evangelization.

Looking back on Pope Benedict's papacy, one thing is clear: those who thought the New Evangelization wasn't a priority for Pope Benedict XVI weren't paying close attention.

~

A cardinal in Latin America, however, was paying close attention.

In an interview with George Weigel in 2012, Jorge Cardinal Bergoglio, the archbishop of Buenos Aires, echoed Benedict, noting:

> The Church is called to a deep and profound rethinking of its mission…. It cannot retreat in response to those who see only confusion, dangers, and threats…. What is required is confirming, renewing, and revitalizing the newness of the Gospel … out of a personal and community encounter with Jesus Christ that raises up disciples and missionaries."[14]

Right now, as the New Evangelization moves into full gear under that cardinal, today known as Pope Francis, you and I are part of a moment for which the Church has been preparing over the better part of a century — a moment that won't pass anytime soon.

That's because the New Evangelization isn't one program or objective among many. Rather, as the Successors of Peter have recognized for more than four decades, the New Evangelization is *the* program, *the* objective, and *the* mission. Every other movement, every other program, apostolate, or ministry is meant to further it. The New Evangelization is the book title. The rest are just chapters and subheadings.

To see that, to see the New Evangelization as the great work of our age, should be to see the New Evangelization as the great work of our lives.

"Should be." Not "is."

Unfortunately, despite all the popes' urgings to take up the work of the New Evangelization, a good many Catholics have politely declined.

# *Chapter 3*

~

# The New Evangelization: A "Catholic Thing"

Not long ago, I put a question to the students in my graduate theology course on the New Evangelization.

"How many of you have brought a person to faith in Christ, from unbelief to baptism?" I asked.

Two hands went up. Out of forty students. And one of those hands belonged to a former missionary.

Admittedly, it was a question I shouldn't have asked. It had a distinctly Protestant flavor to it and, in many ways, missed the point of the New Evangelization, which is about so much more than racking up numbers of souls saved.

Nevertheless, the results of that quick survey pointed to one of the New Evangelization's primary obstacles — namely, that Catholics don't have much experience when it comes to sharing their faith with others. Many are reluctant to do it. So, many don't do it.

Try as they might (and they have tried), the Church's popes, for all their talk about evangelization over the past forty years, have not convinced the majority of people sitting in parish pews on Sundays that evangelization is "a Catholic thing."

That reaction is wrong (and a little surprising) for many reasons, not the least of which is that for the better part of the last two thousand years, Catholics have been all about evangelization. That, after all, is how Christianity spread from a backwater corner of the Roman Empire to much of Europe and a good chunk of Asia and Africa within the first few centuries after Christ's death and Resurrection.

It's also how Christianity came to the New World. Catholic missionaries were among the first to arrive in the Americas, and the desire to spread the faith was one reason King Ferdinand and Queen Isabella underwrote Columbus' voyage in the first place.

Granted, vowed priests and religious, not lay men and women, did most of the initial evangelization of the Americas, but the Catholic laity still shared the Church's enthusiasm for seeing the Gospel made known. They understood that everyone needed the faith, that everyone needed Christ. It wasn't just a private matter between a person and God.

What happened to change that? Why do so many Catholics today think of evangelization as just "a Protestant thing"?

## A LUKEWARM LOVE

There are, I submit, two answers to that question: the simple answer and the more complex answer. Let's start with the simple one: the reticence regarding evangelization stems, at least in part, from a crisis of faith within the Catholic Church.

In both *Verbum Domini* and *Sacramentum Caritatis*, Pope Benedict delicately pointed out that for many years Catholic preaching and teaching was not always what it should have been.

Noting that even now, "the quality of homilies needs to be improved," Benedict also lamented the decades long separation of biblical exegesis and faith "at the highest academic levels" that has given "rise to a lack of clarity in the preparation of homilies" and "can create confusion and a lack of stability in the intellectual formation of candidates for ecclesial ministries."[15]

Practically speaking, that meant that in seminaries, universities, high schools, grade schools, and parish pulpits, the faith wasn't always taught in all its fullness. The full Gospel wasn't preached. Something similar happened in many families. Rather than handing on the faith in the home, parents left the catechizing to Catholic schools, assuming (often incorrectly) that those schools were doing everything necessary to make good Catholics out of their children.

The result of that catechetical breakdown is an overabundance of Catholics who don't know the faith to which they're called to bear witness. Even more fundamentally, they don't understand the importance of that faith. This explains why they're not all that excited about witnessing to it.

When you know Jesus — when you know who he is, what he's done for you, what he's sacrificed for you, what he's given you — it's hard not to be overjoyed. It's also hard not to share all you know with others. You want to tell people about Jesus. You want to tell people about his Church. You want to tell them about the teachings and the graces and the saints and the sacraments and everything you've encountered that has changed who you are. You can't help it. It just flows out of you.

Think of it this way: When we see a good movie or hear a great new band, the first thing most of us do afterward is share it with others. We tell them they've just got to go see this film or listen to this group. If we feel that way about a movie, shouldn't we feel all the more so about the God who became man, died on the cross, and rose again, all so that we could live in eternal happiness with him?

The answer is, of course we should. A true understanding of the gift we have in our Catholic faith should send us to the rooftops, shouting with joy and gratitude the words of the psalmist: "Come and hear, all you who fear God, and I will tell what he has done for me" (Ps 66:16).

The fact that we see so few Catholics shouting from the rooftops tells us that many people sitting in church on Sunday don't know why they're there or what's taking place. They've received the sacraments, but they've never encountered Jesus Christ in a meaningful and personal way. Or the teaching given to them in the past by priests and catechists was so inadequate that they lack confidence in their knowledge and beliefs. Either way, the result is the same: they may have heard the call to evangelize, but it's a call they have no intention of answering.


## STRANGERS IN A FOREIGN LAND

That was the simple answer: many Catholics don't know what they have, so they're not inclined to share it. But the simple answer isn't the only answer.

The catechetical renewal of the last two decades means that more than a few Catholics today do know their faith. Many have encountered Christ and fallen in love with him. But plenty of those Catholics still duck and run for cover when they hear the Church talk about evangelization. The very word makes many Catholics — many faithful, devout Catholics — nervous. Again: Why?

For Catholics in the United States, part of that answer is rooted in our history. Our skepticism about evangelization goes back to our beginnings — when Catholic men and women started making their home in a primarily Protestant country.

Although anti-Catholicism is on the rise again, what we face pales in comparison to what our forebears in the faith faced here in the eighteenth and nineteenth centuries.

For example, before the first shot was fired in the American Revolution, provisions banning Catholics from holding political office existed in most colonial charters. Likewise, for a time, both the colonies of Massachusetts and Virginia forbade Catholics from settling within their territorial boundaries. In other places, Catholic schools, the sacraments, and the Mass itself were banned.

Later, in the nineteenth century, a series of anti-Catholic potboilers, like the utterly false but best-selling *Maria Monk's Awful Disclosures of the Hotel Dieu Nunnery in Montreal*, inflamed hostility against Catholic immigrants. Vandals destroyed parish property, politicians lobbied to exclude Catholics from the Western Territories, and mobs burned at least one convent in Massachusetts to the ground.

Strains of that virulent anti-Catholicism endured well into the twentieth century, with groups like the Ku Klux Klan hating Catholics almost as much as they hated African-Americans.

In the midst of all that, many Catholics decided the best possible thing to do was to keep quiet about their faith and let things be. They wanted to blend in, showing Protestants how "normal" and "American" they were. Not surprisingly, sharing their faith with strangers didn't seem like the best way to accomplish that.

In fact, as a way of showing their Protestant neighbors just how happy they were to "get along," one of the first Catholic seminaries in the United States went so far as to remove the traditional course on evangelization from the seminary curriculum. When other seminaries were founded, they followed suit. As time passed, this left many Catholic priests, as well as the people to whom they ministered, knowing neither what evangelization was nor how to go about it.[16]

## CARICATURES AND CONFUSION

In the second half of the twentieth century, a growing evangelical fervor for spreading the faith has compounded that problem.

As the mainline Protestant churches have declined, evangelical Protestantism — which defines itself by its enthusiasm for spreading the Christian faith — has grown. Countless evangelicals — including myself at one time — have made it their goal in life to convert unbelievers. And in their minds, as often as not, unbelievers include Catholics.

Because of that, many Catholics associate evangelization with the attacks on their faith that have come at them in the past from Protestant co-workers and classmates, or with the overly emotional and manipulative anti-Catholic rhetoric that may have convinced their loved ones to leave the Church.

Other Catholics equate the word "evangelist" with images of televangelists on Sunday morning. It makes them think of oily hucksters asking people to save their souls by writing large checks, or some of them weeping in front of cameras repenting of some personal scandal. Street-corner preachers, Mormons in shirtsleeves and ties, and embezzling pastors of megachurches — those are the only encounters with "evangelists" that many Catholics have had, and those associations stick.

Then, there's the problem of triumphalism.

Triumphalism is the attitude that says, "We Catholics have the one, true faith, possessing the fullness of truth and salvation. Everyone who isn't Catholic is lost. Everyone who is Catholic is found."

Now, it's true that the Church is the one true faith, and that she does possess the fullness of truth and salvation. Nevertheless, when we start treating non-Catholics in a condescending way, presenting the faith in a patronizing mode, or pronouncing judgment on the fate of every person not in full communion with the Church, we commit the error of triumphalism. It's not helpful. It persuades precious few of the truth of the faith, and it fails to convey the Christian charity and mercy we're called to show all men and women.

Following Vatican II, Catholics were warned to guard against this deadly destructive form of spiritual pride. And rightly so. "Pride goes before destruction, and a haughty spirit before a fall" (Prov 16:18). But many Catholics took that warning a little too much to heart. They spent all their time focusing on what was wrong with the Church or how her sons and daughters sinned in the past, and not on learning what was right with the Church or acknowledging how much she had to offer the modern world. The result, as Avery Cardinal Dulles described, is what we see today: that "attempting to be modest and self-critical, [Catholics] often fail to proclaim their faith with confidence, if at all."[17]

Mixed in with all that is the quintessentially American attitude that "religion is a private matter," not a topic of discussion in polite company, as well as the natural reticence to say anything that might give offense or make one unpopular around the office water cooler.

Life in a culture where "tolerance" is the virtue trumpeted before all other virtues only heightens that reticence. Few want to be perceived as saying their beliefs are better than someone else's beliefs. Nor do they want to be perceived as "pressuring" someone to think anything other than what they already think.

Add it all up, and it becomes easier to understand why some Catholics get skittish when they hear talk about evangelization. The combination of confusion and fear is a powerful one. It prevents many Catholic men and women from talking openly about their faith with those who don't share it and letting their "light so shine before men" (Mt 5:16). It prevents even more Catholics from inviting others to learn more about the faith or challenging people to think more deeply about questions of belief.

## A Silent Witness

Plenty of Catholics will deny that of course. They'll say they do bear witness to Christ ... just not with words. Rather, they claim, they bear witness with their lives, heeding St. Francis' advice to "Preach the Gospel always. When necessary, use words."

There are, however, a couple of problems with that line of thinking, starting with this: The saying is a medieval urban legend. If you talk to scholars of Francis' life and work, like the ones I work with at Franciscan University, they'll all tell you the same thing: not a single historical account exists of him saying those words. He certainly lived that way. It captures something of his approach to preaching the Gospel — but not all of his approach. And the words still aren't his.

That's not to say that witness isn't important. It is. It's incredibly important. "Faith by itself, if it has no works, is dead" (Jas 2:17). People need to see us living the faith we proclaim. It's what makes our words credible. It is, in many ways, the heart of evangelization — new or otherwise.

The importance of witness, however, doesn't give us license to dispense with words. Words matter too. They're essential. And the reason they're essential is because none of us are so truly and clearly living the Good News that the witness of our lives is sufficient for bringing people to faith.

As I tell folks when they use this excuse on me, "If you really think your witness is sufficient, that words aren't necessary, go talk to your sister or your spouse and ask them if the witness of your life is so powerful, so moving and complete, that they can just look at you and know everything they could ever possibly need to know about God, Jesus Christ, and the Church, about sin and grace, sanctification, and salvation. Can people see it all in how you live every minute of every day? Could a complete biography of your life replace the Gospels? Or is something, at least occasionally, lacking?"

The answer, obviously, is that something is lacking. A whole lot of somethings are lacking — from my witness, your witness, and the witness of every fallen human being in this world. Even the holiest saints the Church has produced, St. Francis included, needed to use words to lead people to Christ.

The Second Vatican Council's Decree on the Apostolate of the Laity (*Apostolicam Actuositatem*) acknowledged the importance of bearing witness to Christ with our lives, noting that such a witness has "the power to draw men to belief and to God."

But it then goes on to say:

> However, [the lay apostolate] does not consist only in the witness of one's way of life; a true apostle looks for opportunities to announce Christ by words addressed either to non-believers with a view to leading them to faith, or to the faithful with a view to instructing, strengthening, and encouraging them to a more fervent life. "For the charity of Christ impels us" (2 Cor 5:14). The words of the Apostle should echo in all hearts, "Woe to me if I do not preach the Gospel." (n. 6)

~

Again, both words and witness are essential. They work together. They complete each other, making our apostolate effective and whole. The Church doesn't give us the option of picking one over the other. Nor does she give us the option of letting our preference for one mode of evangelization be our excuse for neglecting the other mode.

Instead, she calls us to overcome our reluctance to evangelize and to do it in word and deed. Not just for the sake of others, but for our own sake as well.

# *Chapter 4*

## ~

# THE NEW EVANGELIZATION: A MISSION FOR THE WHOLE CHURCH

ONE OF THE GREAT GIFTS IN BEING CATHOLIC is the lack of guesswork involved. Through his Church, God has charted out the course that leads to him, and, as baptized believers, we just have to follow that course.

True, we don't know every step we'll need to take or every obstacle we'll encounter along the way. The journey to holiness is full of surprises. Nevertheless, the general way is clear. It includes participating in the Mass and receiving the sacraments, being kind to our neighbor, caring for the poor, and respecting the dignity of the human person in all our thoughts and actions.

It also includes evangelizing.

When it comes to individual Catholic's duty to evangelize, the *Catechism of the Catholic Church* doesn't mince words.

Quoting *Lumen Gentium* (the Second Vatican Council's Dogmatic Constitution on the Church), paragraph 1285 of the *Catechism* describes the baptized and confirmed as "true witnesses of Christ," and states that all Catholics are "strictly obliged to spread and defend the faith by word and deed."[18]

"Strictly obliged" is strong language. It doesn't leave much room for doubt about what the Church expects of her members. No matter how much we might prefer to leave the heavy lifting to the ordained and consecrated, the Church doesn't give us that option. She says the work belongs to the laity, as much as it does to priests and religious.

There are two reasons for that. The first is this: when we evangelize others, we evangelize ourselves.

## EVANGELIZING THE EVANGELIZERS

Let's go back for a moment to that phrase from the *Catechism* — "strictly obliged." That's our clue that something critically important hangs in the balance.

The Church, after all, doesn't "strictly oblige" Catholics to do anything for the fun of it. The things she strictly obliges us to do — participate in the Mass, go to confession, fast on Ash Wednesday and Good Friday — she does for our own good, because those actions are essential to our quest for holiness.

Evangelization is no different. The Church strictly obliges Catholics to share the faith because we need to share it. We need to evangelize.

In *Redemptoris Missio*, Pope John Paul II summed up the reasoning behind that need, writing, "*Faith is strengthened when it is given to others!*" (n. 2; emphasis in the original).

It's not difficult to see how that works.

When you step out on a limb and begin to share your faith — when you make it known at work or the gym that you take your Catholic identity seriously — you will get questions. People will say things to you like "I used to be Catholic, but I don't see why I need a priest coming between me and God" or "How can you be Catholic when the Church is so opposed to science?" There's also the perennial favorite: "Why do Catholics worship Mary?"

Sometimes, you'll know the answers. Other times, you won't. And when people start throwing questions at you that catch you off guard, one of two things usually happens: You either stop talking about your faith, or you go find out the answers.

If you choose the latter course of action, you don't return to the conversation the same. You come back knowing more and understanding more. You come back with a fuller realization of who Christ is and what the Church teaches. In the process of explaining the faith, you learn about the faith.

That's true with teaching anything. When you have to explain an idea to others, you come to know it better yourself. When you have to boil down an idea to its essence, you learn to focus on the essentials, on what matters most, and then go from there.

So, when teaching someone about the American Revolution, you don't waste time talking about the design of the Continental Army's uniforms or the battle maneuvers employed at small skirmishes. Rather, you talk about the fundamental principles for which the colonists fought and the major figures and turning points that led to the defeat of the British army. You talk about freedom and self-determination, George Washington and John Adams, the Boston Massacre and Valley Forge.

Similarly, when sharing the Gospel, you focus on the basic Christian message, the core of the Good News — who Christ is, what he offers us, and why we need what he offers. That is the *kerygma*, the essential Christian message restated by St. Paul so many times in his epistles:

> For I delivered to you as of first importance what I also received, that Christ died for our sins in accordance with the Scriptures, that he was buried, that he was raised on the third day in accordance with the Scriptures, and that he appeared to Cephas, then to the Twelve.... For as by a man came death, by a man has come also the resurrection of the dead. For as in Adam all die, so also in Christ shall all be made alive. (1 Cor 15:3-5, 21-23)

## THE WORLD'S GREATEST LOVE STORY

Evangelization helps us to avoid majoring in the minors, keeping us focused on what is most essential to the faith. In that, we discover what is of supreme importance and universal value. We see the need for the Gospel, how it touches people, how it speaks to people, and how it applies to men and women of every age, class, and race.

Once we grasp the universal validity of the message and its significance for the whole of human life, we gain a new appreciation both for it and for what it means to bear that message. That, in turn, gives us a new eagerness to share it. We realize the Good News is too great to keep to ourselves. We need to share it with all those who need to hear it. And everyone needs to hear it.

Focusing on the essentials of the Gospel also helps change the nature of our faith. We stop thinking of it as something we're obliged to believe — as a cultural patrimony inherited from our parents and grandparents — and start seeing it as a loving relationship with a Person, with Jesus Christ.

Jesus Christ isn't just part of the Good News; he *is* the Good News. Likewise, a relationship with him isn't just part of our Catholic faith; it *is* our Catholic faith. Everything else about being Catholic — the sacraments and saints, priests and rosaries, holy water and the Bible itself — serves to facilitate that relationship. They're gifts meant to help us know and love him better, to help us draw closer to him and share in his life. The more we share our faith, the more we come to understand that. And the more we understand that, the more we start to think like the Church's greatest saints have always thought.

When you read Augustine and John of the Cross, Teresa of Ávila and Thérèse of Lisieux, you're reading the story of a great love affair, the love affair all of those saints had with Jesus. The Church's greatest mystics are the men and women who fell most completely in love with God.

Note how that love didn't lead them away from the Church's sacramental and devotional life. Those saints didn't say, "I have Jesus; I don't need a priest or Mary or the Mass." Rather, that love led them more deeply into the sacramental and devotional life of the Church. They came to understand those things from the inside out, seeing them not as obligations or dispensable extras but as precious gifts and powerful helps in their journey to God.

The same holds true for us. The closer we grow to Jesus and the more we come to love him, the more we come to understand all the rest that the Church teaches and offers us. In turn, the more we understand them, the more we embrace those things, giving thanks to God for providing so much help for his needy children along the way.

In all that, we find joy. We become the joyful witnesses the world needs, knowing our faith and living it with a clarity that draws others to Christ.

### WALKING THE TALK

Sharing our faith with others strengthens our knowledge of the faith, thereby transforming our witness. But that's not the only way it transforms our witness.

Back in college, I took a summer job working on a loading dock. The guys I worked with weren't the godliest bunch of men, and as the weeks passed, their worldliness started to rub off on me. I didn't take the work seriously, and I loafed on the job. I also kept my faith to myself. I didn't talk about being Christian.

It took about a month, but one morning, walking across the bridge into the city, I decided that needed to change. I asked God to help me find an opportunity to share my faith with my co-workers. And sure enough, without even looking for it, an opportunity came along almost that very hour.

Almost as soon as the words were out of my mouth, however, I realized my attitude on the job would have to change as well. I knew that if I wanted the witness of my words to reach them, the witness of my life had better match those words. It didn't matter how the other guys talked or acted. Their behavior couldn't be the standard anymore. In sharing my faith, I'd set a new standard, one all my own.

The same holds true for all Christians who let their faith be known. Sharing Christ with others isn't like sharing stock tips or a recipe for apple pie. It's an inherently personal witness in which we put ourselves out front and center as a living testimony to the truth we share. Our actions become accountable to our words. Expectations change. And we feel the pressure to change along with those expectations.

Every once in a while, that pressure can be a bad thing. It can lead people into the sin of hypocrisy, acting one way in the light and another way in the dark. More often than not, however, it just serves as a gentle reminder that our lives are not our own, and that we're called to clear a higher bar than the one the world sets for us. It spurs us on to greater things, helping us keep our temper or tongue or other disordered impulses in check.

Not that we'll always accomplish those greater things. Jesus Christ or no Jesus Christ, we're still fallen human beings, which means we will have days when our temper gets the better of us or when our selfish preoccupation with our own problems blinds us to the needs of others. Aiming high doesn't mean we'll always hit our target. But we will hit it far more often than if we never aim for it at all. Likewise, the more we aim for it, the more we'll hit it.

In the moral life, as with most everything else, practice (almost) makes perfect.

## A CULTURE IN NEED

In calling for Catholics to more eagerly share the faith, the popes of our time have hit upon an effective remedy to the Church's present ills. Through sharing the faith, faith grows. Through teaching the faith, the faith is understood. And through witnessing to the faith, our witness is perfected.

If we Catholics today are sometimes weak in our faith, that at least partly stems from our reluctance to share it. The more we keep the Good News to ourselves, the less "good" that news seems. We're tempted to stop seeing it for what it is — a message true and essential for every human life and for the whole of human life — and instead start seeing it as a message true just for us.

Catholics can't afford to think that way. Not today. Not in this culture.

Catholics need to evangelize because our personal faith will wither on the vine if we don't share it. But we also need to evangelize because the culture and the men and women within it need the faith we have to share.

Remember how at the beginning of this chapter I said there were two reasons why the New Evangelization was a task for the whole Church, not just for the ordained and consecrated? Well, here's the second reason: Because priests and religious cannot go where the laity can go. They cannot reach the people we can reach.

A few generations back, you can understand why many Catholics didn't see the need to evangelize. They could live their faith in their homes and parishes, and when they walked outside — going to work or school or the playground — the cultural temperature didn't feel that much different than it felt inside. For all appearances, the gap between the Catholic way of life and the American way of life didn't look that great.

Today, however, when Catholics walk outside our homes and parishes into the culture at large, we feel the difference. It hits us in the face like a slap of ice-cold wind. The culture has turned toxic, and the gap between how the Church calls us to live and how the culture tells us to live has grown so wide, we can no longer bridge it.

But while we can't bridge the gap, we can attempt to close it. That's what the New Evangelization calls us to do. It calls us to transform not just individuals but the entire culture, recognizing that just as the de-Christianization of culture led countless men and women away from the Church, so can the re-Christianization of culture lead men and women back to the Church.

That's what we're doing when we share our faith, through both our silent and spoken witness, with the people in our neighborhoods and communities, schools and workplaces. We're transforming the culture by introducing the individuals within it to a Person who will transform the very fabric of their lives. We're also welcoming them into a family of believers who will walk with them as they strive to live the life to which God calls them.

## A Culture in Crisis

That's something your parish priest can't do. He can't bear witness to the guy in your office who has never stepped foot in a Catholic Church. He can't strike up a conversation at the gym or the coffee shop with the person who stopped going to Mass a decade ago. Your priest's reach is limited. The sisters who teach in the parish schools or work at the local hospital have the same limited reach. They can do great things where they are. They can do great things with their prayers and sacrifices as well. But they can't go where you can go.

Vatican II's Decree on the Apostolate of the Laity spells that out, explaining that the Catholic laity "share in the priestly, prophetic, and royal office of Christ and therefore have their own share in the mission of the whole people of God...."

It then goes on to tell us how exactly we are to share in that mission: through "activity directed to the evangelization and sanctification of men and to the penetrating and perfecting of the temporal order through the spirit of the Gospel." Lastly, it tells us where that activity needs to take place: "in the midst of the world and its concerns" we are to carry out our apostolate "like leaven, with the ardor of the spirit of Christ" (n. 2).

Make no mistake, people need us to be that leaven. They need our witness.

They need to know who they are — that they have a dignity that doesn't depend on how they look or what they do or how much they earn.

They need to know truth exists, and they need to know how to live in accord with that truth.

They also need to know that God exists — a God who created them, loves them, and wants to love them for an eternity.

They need to know that God gave them a Church, a family, which offers them a healing that goes beyond pharmaceuticals, and which comes to them through the sacraments.

They need to know that God gives them his own body and blood as food, and his own family as their family.

They need to know how to live as husbands and wives, mothers and fathers, brothers and sisters, honoring God's perfect plan for how to love and giving thanks for all of the gifts he's given them to help them follow that plan.

They need to know all that in order to find the peace and joy and happiness for which they long, for which they were made. And the only place they can find all that is the Catholic Church.

~

Our work in the New Evangelization is to lead men and women to those truths. That work, however, is more than the work of a moment.

Which brings us to the last misconception about the New Evangelization we need to tackle: that evangelization is simply a onetime proclamation of the Gospel.

# Chapter 5

## ~

# THE NEW EVANGELIZATION: THE WORK OF A LIFETIME

It was a sentence that caught me by surprise.

In 2003, Pope John Paul II published the encyclical letter *Ecclesia de Eucharistia* (on the Eucharist in relation to the Church). In it, he wrote, "The Eucharist thus appears as both *the source* and *the summ*it of all evangelization" (n. 22; emphasis in the original).

When I first read those words, I didn't understand what he meant. Like many Catholics and most Protestants, I tended to think of evangelization as the initial proclamation of the Gospel or bringing someone to belief in Christ. Introducing somebody to Jesus as the Savior meant proclaiming the *kerygma* — helping them understand that (1) God loves us, (2) we have sinned, (3) Christ has died and risen to save us, and (4) we have to respond with faith.

Receiving the sacraments, however, seemed another thing altogether. As a Catholic, I couldn't walk up to somebody, share the Gospel, then take him to church to receive Communion with me that same day.

So how do you base evangelization, new or otherwise, on the Eucharist?

My confusion only grew when, a few weeks later, I came across a talk that Francis Cardinal George had presented years earlier at a conference for Catholic scholars. He began the talk with the following words: "The bulk of what I am about to say is simply an extended footnote on a single sentence. All evangelizers proclaim who Christ is. Catholic evangelizers proclaim a Eucharistic Christ."[19]

Then, I discovered that Pope Benedict XVI, when he was still Cardinal Ratzinger, had said much the same thing.

Addressing a group of catechists gathered in Rome, he commented on the structure and content of the New Evangelization. "The Church always evangelizes and has never interrupted the path of evangelization," he said. "She celebrates the eucharistic mystery every day, administers the sacraments, proclaims ... the Word of God.... And this evangelization bears fruit."[20]

What did those words mean? Was it just ecclesiastical rhetoric?

No, it wasn't. It's the heart and soul of the Gospel according to the Catholic Church.

## EVANGELIZATION'S ENDGAME

As evangelical Protestants see it, the goal of evangelization is leading someone to belief in Christ, a belief expressed through what they call the Sinner's Prayer, which goes something like this: "Lord, thank you for your love, I admit that I have sinned, but I confess that Jesus died for my sins, and I want to give my life for him as he gave his life for me."

That's not to say they believe a person's faith journey ends with the Sinner's Prayer. A life of belief — reading the Bible, going to church, obeying the commandments — should follow. Nevertheless, once someone prays that prayer, evangelicals consider the deal done. Once saved, always saved.

For Catholics, however, it's a bit more complicated.

Just getting someone to say the Sinner's Prayer isn't enough. It's beautiful. It's essential. But it isn't sufficient. It's only the first step of the Prodigal Son on his journey back to his Father's house. It's not the final destination. It's not the endgame.

The endgame is heaven. And the way we get there is through the Eucharist. It's through our full participation in the Body of Christ, receiving God' own life through the sacraments.

That's what John Paul II meant when he said that evangelization must be based on the Eucharist. The more I contemplated his words, the more I came to see that he was drawing from the wisdom of the Church Fathers, who understood evangelization not as a transaction — where we offer an idea to someone and they either buy it or don't buy it — but rather as a divine romance played out over the course of a lifetime in the liturgical, sacramental, and devotional life of the Church.

## An Evangelization in Three Parts

To understand this more fully, we need to look back at the witness of the early Catholic evangelists — those tasked with proclaiming the Gospel to a pre-Christian culture in the first few centuries after Christ.

If we study the strategy of the early Church, we see that to those first Christians, evangelization had a much richer mean-

ing than simply bringing someone to faith. Those same four
basic steps — getting someone to recognize that God loves
them, that they've sinned, that Christ died for their sins, and
that they must respond by faith — were there. They saw those
four steps, however, as just the initial evangelization that led
to the initial decision. The end result, if someone made that
decision and came to believe in Christ, wasn't to say, "That's it.
Evangelization complete. Once saved, always saved."

Instead, the way you expressed your commitment to
Christ as a new believer was to move from step one — becoming a convert — to step two — becoming a catechumen.
You had the sign of the cross made over you, salt sprinkled on
you, hands laid upon you, and the prayers of exorcism said.
Then you enrolled in the Order of the Catechumenate. Having been evangelized, you now needed to be catechized.

In the early Church, the catechumenate might last an entire year or even more. For St. Cyprian, it lasted almost three
years.

In his writing, Cyprian admits that when he heard the
Gospel, came to faith, and realized what the Church taught —
what Jesus expected — he was skeptical. He didn't think anyone like him could live like that. So he stayed at that second
stage — not simply as a convert who had been evangelized,
but as a catechumen being catechized. During that time, he
learned the creed, he learned the Lord's Prayer, and eventually
he began to see that God didn't ask him to live the faith all
on his own steam. He didn't have to do it by himself. Rather,
the Holy Spirit would empower him, just as he empowered
all those Cyprian saw living the Christian faith around him.[21]

When Cyprian realized that, he resolved to finish stage
two as a catechumen and move on to stage three. He had been
catechized. Now it was time to be sacramentalized.

This stage began when the catechumen went to the Easter Vigil and became a communicant. You were baptized, con-

firmed, and received your First Holy Communion. At that point, empowered by the Holy Spirit, you were introduced to the deepest mysteries of the faith: the sacraments.

The early Church called this introduction "mystagogy" — meaning, "guidance into the mysteries." From Easter until Pentecost and beyond, the Church instructed the newly baptized and confirmed in the deepest truths of the faith: the sacraments. Before the Easter Vigil, they didn't learn about what Christ does for us in the sacraments. That's because the Church Fathers believed those truths were so beautiful, so overwhelming, that until the sacraments themselves transformed the new communicants, they couldn't understand them. The sacraments wouldn't make any sense, the Fathers held, without the help of the Holy Spirit.

## AN EVANGELIZATION FOR THE WHOLE PERSON

In St. Justin Martyr's *First Apology*, he sums up that process of instruction, writing:

> As many are persuaded and believe what we teach and say is true, and undertake to be able to live accordingly, they are instructed to pray and entreat God with fasting for the remission of their sins. They are then brought, by us, where there is water and are regenerated in the same manner in which we ourselves were reborn as children of God.[22]

Let's unpack that.

First, "many are persuaded." That results from the initial proclamation.

Second, "and believe what we teach and say is true." That comes from catechizing.

Third, and finally, they "are regenerated in the same manner in which we ourselves were reborn as children of God." That is the reception of the sacraments and the beginning of the instruction in the mysteries of the faith.

Note how the will is addressed in evangelizing, the intellect is strengthened in catechizing, and both are prepared to submit to and understand even deeper truths through fasting and prayer.

That's how the early Church understood evangelization: as a process that involved the whole person — mind, body, and spirit — and which unfolded, through the coordination of all three, over the course of many years.

The Church Fathers saw evangelization in that light because they knew what the Church still knows: the Good News isn't exhausted in the proclamation of Christ as Lord and Savior. Nor is the reception of Baptism, Confirmation, and Communion the end of the Christian journey. The reception of the sacraments isn't the end of being catechized any more than it is the end of being evangelized. It's just a more glorious beginning. The deeper you go, the better the Good News gets. It becomes almost too good to believe.

## AN EVANGELIZATION OF DIVINE ROMANCE

To understand the internal logic of this threefold process, we only have to think of what it feels like to fall in love. In a sense, those three stages of entering into the life of Christ — evangelizing, catechizing, and sacramentalizing — match up to the three stages of romance: courtship, engagement, and marriage.

Many years ago, when I was still in college, I got up the nerve to ask Kimberly Kirk on a date. I knew right away that she was special, that she was different from every other girl I had met. And as we got to know each other better, we began to fall in love.

But it didn't stop there. It started. It started with that personal relationship. Then, one evening in January 1979, with the snow falling, I got down on my knees and asked her to be my wife. At that point, we moved from stage one — courtship — to stage two — engagement. During that time, she really had to learn the ways of this man. And I had to learn the truth of the old maxim — that you don't just marry the girl; you marry her whole family. We were engaged for many months, and it was the best and worst of both worlds. We enjoyed being in love and knowing we were destined to be married, but at the same time we didn't want that time to last forever. We longed for more.

That more came the following August, when we moved to the third and final step: marital communion. After that, whole new worlds opened up to both of us. We learned things and understood things about each other and the Sacrament of Marriage that we never could have understood during courtship and engagement. I fell more deeply in love with Kimberly as her husband than I ever could have as her boyfriend or fiancé. And I still am falling more deeply in love with her. I still am learning about her and growing in my understanding of her. That's how marriage works. You don't stop loving and learning on your wedding day. You start loving and learning in a whole new way.

The same holds true for evangelization.

Just like with courtship, the Christian journey doesn't end with evangelization. It starts there. Just like with engagement, knowing the faith isn't enough for a believing Christian, you long for more: you long to enter into a covenantal, familial relationship. And just like with marriage, the reception of the sacraments isn't the end of the journey. It's only the beginning.

Having enjoyed the nuptial bath and partaken of the Wedding Feast of the Supper of the Lamb, you are empowered to know and love God in a way that was impossible before. And that knowing and loving doesn't end in a day. It doesn't end in a lifetime.

This vision of evangelization as a threefold process of falling in love, committing to love, and growing in love is what John Paul II describes in his landmark document on the teaching of the faith, *Catechesi Tradendae* ("On Catechesis in Our Time"), where he writes that "catechesis is a moment or aspect of evangelization" (n. 26).

The *Catechism* describes something similar when it tells us: "The entire Christian life bears the mark of the spousal love of Christ and the Church. Already Baptism, the entry into the People of God, is a nuptial mystery; it is so to speak the nuptial bath (cf. Eph 5:26-27), which precedes the wedding feast, the Eucharist" (CCC 1617).

Knowing and loving in that way, of course, doesn't come easily. Not long ago, a young man came up to me at a conference and mentioned how reluctant he was to marry the woman he lived with. "Things are so good right now," he told me. "I just think getting married would complicate things."

To a point, he was right. Marriage does complicate things. Becoming part of a family is difficult. Personal relationships, on the other hand, are comparatively easy. When it's just you and the one you love, it's neater. It's tidy. It's simple. Introducing parents and siblings and cousins and all the dynamics of family adds whole levels of complications. But it also makes the experience so much richer, so much more fulfilling. And you can't really know the one you love without also knowing their family too. Their family helped make them who they are.

What's true of human love is even truer of divine love. Calling people simply to a personal relationship with Jesus is easy. Calling them to a Church, to the sacraments, to all that the Catholic Church asks of us — all of this adds complications. But the Catholic Church's way of evangelizing fits what God is doing as a Father, through his Son, in a family. That's what we are. We're not just a megachurch or an independent congregation. We're a worldwide family, and there are a lot of people to meet in God's family. There's something irresistible about that. It adds complications. But it also adds a beauty and richness that is almost indescribable.

## AN EVANGELIZATION THAT EMPOWERS

Minutes before Jesus ascended to his Father, he said to his disciples: "Go therefore and make disciples of all nations, baptizing them in the name of the Father and of the Son and of the Holy Spirit, teaching them to observe all that I have commanded you" (Mt 28:19-20).

The command to "Go" speaks to the initial proclamation, the outward movement of the disciple into the world, proclaiming the Good News. "[T]eaching them to observe all that I have commanded you" is the work of catechesis. And "baptizing" points to the sacramental element of the New Evangelization, the call to bring all the peoples of the earth into the family of God.

That is why evangelization must be based on the Eucharist.

The Eucharist helps us understand that proclaiming those four fundamentals we talked about earlier can never be enough. Those who do that have their hearts in the right place, but they're not following through on the fullness of the Great Commission. They're only proclaiming a half-truth — or, more accurately, a third of the truth. They've truncated the meaning of evangelization to a single moment, just as they've truncated the meaning of what it means to follow Christ to a single yes.

Both evangelization and the faith itself are so much bigger than that. And the Eucharist shows us that. The Eucharist is, as *Lumen Gentium* said, "the source and the summit of the Christian life" (n. 11). Again, it's the endgame. It propels us through the stages of evangelization and catechesis to the Marriage Supper of the Lamb. It then empowers us to grow in love and faith every day of our Catholic lives, compelling us to share that faith with others.

When we understand that, we understand the scope of the New Evangelization. We see the fullness of the faith we're tasked to share, and we see the fullness of the relationship to which we're called.

~

In Galilee long ago, Jesus called Simon Peter to himself again and again: when Peter, with his brother Andrew, first came to see Jesus; when Jesus borrowed Peter's boat to preach from the water; when Peter's nets burst with fish; when Peter walked on water; when Jesus talked with Peter on the beach after the Resurrection.

Each call was a call to a deeper level of faith, a deeper level of trust.

As Peter moved through that succession of calls, he learned more about Jesus and himself. He learned what he could do when he trusted God. And he learned that for all his faith, he could still betray the One he loved. His every yes became a lesson in humility, a humility that eventually enabled him to receive the power to draw others to Christ.

Each of us must walk the same path as Peter.

Every day, in the ordinary circumstances of our lives, Christ calls us to himself. There isn't one call. There are many. And one yes does not a disciple make. The Christian life is a perpetual yes — yes to God's law, yes to God's will, yes to

God's grace. The more yes's we give, the more our love grows. And the more our love grows, the more we find ourselves living as evangelizing Catholics, sharing the faith, proclaiming God's love.

That's true for those who've been part of the family all their lives, as much as it's true for those just discovering the family for the first time.

You see, just as there are plenty of married couples who've fallen out of love with their spouses, there are plenty of sacramentalized Catholics who need to learn to love God all over again. There are others who need to learn to love him for the first time. That's what we mean when we say that the New Evangelization is about evangelizing the baptized. It's about helping them to know and live the fullness of their baptismal vows.

The question for us now becomes: How do we do that? What does a yes to the work of the New Evangelization entail?

# PART II

~

# THE RESPONSE:
# MODELS AND METHODS
# FOR THE
# NEW EVANGELIZATION

*Chapter 6*

~

# THE CATHOLIC GOSPEL:
# LESSONS FROM THE
# FIRST EVANGELISTS

THE NEW EVANGELIZATION ISN'T AS NEW AS WE THINK.

On the one hand, we've been charged to conduct an evangelization that is "new in ardor, new in methods, and new in expression." But the primary task we face — to proclaim Christ and live what we proclaim — is as old as the Church. It's what Christians have been striving to do since Christ ascended into heaven. In carrying out this task, therefore, we aren't completely on our own. We have guides: those who first took the Good News to the highways and byways of the ancient world, as well as the records they wrote.

Those records are the Gospels.

There is a reason we call the writers of the four Gospels "the four evangelists." It's not just because they wrote an *evangelium*, a Gospel, but also because their proclamation of the life and teaching, death and resurrection, of Jesus was *the*

61

*evangel, the* Gospel. That's what they were — bringers of the Good News.

In the books they wrote, we find both the message and the method of the old evangelization spelled out in black and white. And in that, particularly in the Gospels of Matthew and John, we also find the beginnings of a blueprint for the New Evangelization.

## LESSON 1: PROCLAIM A PERSON

For the first thousand years of the Church's history, one Gospel was read, studied, and written about more than any other: the Gospel of Matthew. Christians of earlier ages recognized it as a work of great literary artistry. They also recognized how it makes Jesus almost immediately present.

From the opening chapters, where Matthew quotes the prophet Isaiah — "Behold, a virgin shall conceive and bear a son, and his name shall be called Emmanuel (which means, God with us)" — to the last words in the last chapter — "And behold, I am with you always, to the close of the age" — Jesus seems to leap off every page (Mt 1:23, 28:20). He is, in Matthew's Gospel as in the world, abidingly present.

That combination gives Matthew's Gospel tremendous power. It reminds us that our task in the New Evangelization, first and foremost, is to proclaim a Person. Not a philosophy. Not a theology. Not even the four spiritual laws. Our task is to proclaim Jesus. The man. His life. His words. Even his manners and idiosyncrasies. That's what Matthew does. He brings us to an encounter with the God who loves us and shows us how he loved us. That was the goal of the first evangelization, and it needs to remain the goal of the New Evangelization.

As Pope Benedict writes in the opening paragraphs of his apostolic exhortation *Verbum Domini*:

I encourage all the faithful to renew their personal and communal encounter with Christ, the word of life made visible, and to become his heralds.... Indeed, sharing in the life of God, a Trinity of love, is *complete joy* (cf. 1 Jn 1:4). And it is the Church's gift and unescapable duty to communicate that joy, born of an encounter with the person of Christ, the Word of God in our midst.... There is no greater priority than this: to enable the people of our time once more to encounter God, the God who speaks to us and shares his love so that we might have life in abundance (cf. Jn 10:10). (n. 2; emphasis in the original)

## LESSON 2: PROCLAIM BY WORDS AND DEEDS

In order to accomplish that, however, words aren't enough. Nor are actions. We need both. And we know we need both because Jesus taught us as much. Matthew shows us that through the structure of his Gospel.

The Gospel of Matthew begins with a prologue about Jesus' origins and ends with an epilogue about his passion, death, and resurrection. The rest of the Gospel is built around five narrative discourses: The Sermon on the Mount in Matthew 5-7, the Mission Discourse in Matthew 10, the seven parables of the Kingdom in Matthew 13, the discourse on the Church in chapters 16-18, and the extended discourse which took place both in the Temple and on the Mount of Olives in Matthew 21-24.

Paired with each of those discourses is an account of Jesus' deeds. In the Gospel of Matthew, Jesus never just speaks. He also prays, heals, patiently endures slander and opposition, raises the dead, and cleanses the Temple.

In the pairing of the two — words and deeds — Matthew reminds us on one level that the Gospel can't be proclaimed with just words, nor can it be proclaimed solely by witness. The two must go together. They must be inseparable.

When Jesus first proclaimed the Kingdom, no separation existed between his words and deeds. Jesus never was content to just perform signs or preach sermons. Nor should we be. When proclaiming the Good News, we must pair our words with deeds, and our deeds must back up our words. Again, both are necessary. Our personal witness presents the faith as a living whole. It prevents the teaching of the faith from lapsing into a fragmented bundle of doctrines, separated from Christ and one another. At the same time, teaching the doctrines of the faith ensures that the whole faith — not just our personal experience of it — is handed on.

That's what Pope Paul VI highlights in *Evangelii Nuntiandi*, noting, "Modern man listens more willingly to witnesses than to teachers, and if he does listen to teachers, it is because they are witnesses" (n. 41).

On another level, in the pairing of the two — words and deeds — Matthew reminds us of one of the fundamental truths about God's Word, made known to us from the beginning: The Word of God doesn't simply inform. It performs. And transforms.

This was true at the Creation, when God said, "Let there be light" (Gen 1:3). He spoke a word, but it wasn't just a word. It was a word that accomplished something. It brought something into being. It was also true at the Last Supper. Jesus said, "This is my body" (Mt 26:26). But he didn't just speak those words. The words accomplished something. Bread became Body.

The same holds true for us today. Whether we're reading the Gospel or proclaiming the Gospel, we're not just reading or speaking words that are informative. Rather, those words are performative and transformative. They always accomplish something. They always do something. They are always, in and of themselves, active, transforming hearts and lives and entire cultures wherever they are faithfully proclaimed. We need to trust that, knowing that despite our limitations, our proclamation of God's Word will always, in some way, accomplish something. It doesn't depend just on us.

## LESSON 3: PROCLAIM THE CHURCH

Matthew's Gospel holds a third important lesson for the New Evangelization: the indispensability of the Church.

Of the four evangelists, Matthew is the only one to explicitly reference the Church. Twice we hear Christ speak the word *ecclesia*: "On this rock I will build my Church," and "If he refuses to listen even to the Church, let him be to you as a Gentile or a tax collector" (Mt 16:18, 18:17).

Those two passages tell us that the Church is an essential part of Jesus' evangelistic mission, endowed not only with the power to preach the Gospel and perform miracles but also with a divine authority. They first do that by helping us see that the Kingdom referenced throughout Matthew's Gospel is one and the same with the Church.

After all, Christ isn't giving Peter two different jobs when he says to him, "On this rock I will build my Church," then "I will give you the keys of the kingdom of heaven, and whatever you bind on earth shall be bound in heaven and whatever you loose on earth shall be loosed in heaven" (Mt 16:18-19). The two tasks go together, because the Church and the Kingdom aren't two separate institutions or entities. Rather, they are inseparably connected.

That connection, between Kingdom and Church, King and Kingdom, likewise establishes the Church's authority.

Think again about Matthew 18:17: "If he refuses to listen *even* to the Church" [emphasis mine]. Jesus' words seem to imply that not listening to the Church is virtually unthinkable. In his mind, the Church is something to which men must listen, to which they *need* to listen. To not listen to the Church is to not listen to those the King has put in charge of the Kingdom, which is the same as not listening to the Kingdom. He recognizes that some will not listen to the Church no matter what, but that doesn't diminish the Church's authority over them. That authority is its by right — again a right entrusted to it by the King.

The Gospel is Christ the King. But it's also Christ the King's Body. It's his Church. They were inseparable in the Gospels, and they are inseparable now. This is why to fail to proclaim the Church — to fail to proclaim her teachings, to fail to proclaim her authority, to fail to proclaim her nature as God's worldwide family that the Father sent the Son to establish by the Spirit — is to fail to proclaim the fullness of the Catholic Gospel.

## LESSON 4:
### PROCLAIM THE FULFILLMENT OF THE COVENANT

The ancient Jewish people knew that their relationship with God was unlike that of every other nation. They didn't just worship God; they belonged to God, as a son belongs to his father. They were God's family, his children by adoption, their relationship forged long before Christ's coming through a sacred bond of kinship known as a covenant.

With the coming of Christ, God's covenant with Israel wasn't abolished. It was fulfilled. How?

Well, as he preached, Jesus again and again relied on familial language — father, son, brother, sister, firstborn, inheritance — to convey the truth about the Kingdom of God. He himself called God "Father" and "*Abba*" (or "Daddy"). To us this is old news. We're so used to hearing God spoken about in such a way that we don't even blink when we come across it in Scripture. But that wasn't the case when Jesus first spoke those words.

In the Sermon on the Mount alone, Jesus refers to God as "Father" seventeen times, a term used only eleven times in the entirety of the Hebrew canon. Jesus' use of kinship language functionally replaces covenant language, which practically disappears in the New Testament. The word "covenant" appears only once in Matthew and Mark, twice in Luke, and not at all in John. Why? Because the reality to which the covenant points — divine sonship — is precisely what the Incarnation achieves.

It can help to think of it this way: By nature, God is not our Father. He is our Creator. We are his creatures. According to nature, therefore, we are his servants, his slaves, and his property. We're no more his children by nature than the books we write or the tomatoes we grow are our children.

But by grace, by Christ assuming our nature and infusing his life — sanctifying grace — into our souls through the sacraments, we can become God's children. He can become our Father. The apostle John can barely contain his wonder at that when he writes, "See what love the Father has given us, that we should be called children of God; and so we are" (1 Jn 3:1).

John in particular drives that point home by building his Gospel around the number seven. In John, Jesus performs seven signs, makes seven "I AM" statements about his own identity, and carries out his ministry within the context of seven liturgical feasts. That focus on the number seven can seem strange to us, but it would have made perfect sense to John's Jewish readers.

For Jews, the Sabbath was the sign of the covenant. It's the day hallowed, made holy, by God's rest. As such, they believed that the Sabbath revealed the goal of creation — the consecration of the world and everything in it to God. Because the Sabbath was the seventh day in the creation cycle, the number seven took on covenantal significance, to the point that in Hebrew, the word for "to swear a covenant" is *shevah*, literally "to seven oneself."

By building his Gospel around the number seven, John reminded the Jews of Jesus' day of their covenant with God and showed them that the reality to which the covenant always pointed — divine sonship — was achieved through the Incarnation.

We'll talk more about this in chapter 12. For now, however, what's important to note is this: In the New Evangelization, we aren't primarily calling people to become part of an organization or institution. Nor are we calling them merely to a personal relationship with Jesus. Rather, we're calling them to a covenant family. We're calling them to divine sonship, to divine kinship, to a reality that our great forefathers in the faith — Abraham, Isaac, and Jacob — couldn't have fathomed.

And what is the way we enter that family, participate in the family life, and receive the grace to enjoy such a great gift? That happens through the sacraments.

## Lesson 5: Proclaim the Sacraments

The early Church, as we already discussed, knew that evangelization wasn't one moment. Rather, they understood it as a lifelong journey lived out in the context of the sacraments. As such, they also knew that sacraments are essential to the life of faith. They are what give us the power to live as disciples of Christ. That's why they viewed evangelization as a threefold process — falling in love, committing to love, and growing in love.

That process, however, wasn't their own. They learned it from St. John, who in turn learned it from Christ.

John writes about this process in the opening passages of his Gospel: "But to all who received him, who believed in his name, he gave power to become children of God" (Jn 1:12).

To receive him is the first moment in evangelization; it's the assent of faith. To believe in his name is the second moment of evangelization; it's to learn more about who Jesus is and what he teaches through his Church in the *Catechism* and the creed. And to receive "power to become children of God" is the third moment of evangelization; it's to receive God's own life in the sacraments so that we can live the lives to which he calls us.

We see that same formula repeated in John 2 and 3. There we're told that when Jesus was in Jerusalem "many believed in his name when they saw the signs which he did; but Jesus did not trust himself to them … for he himself knew what was in man" (Jn 2:23, 25). So people believed, but something was still missing. Belief wasn't enough. We learn more about that "what" in the very next verse when we're introduced to Exhibit A of this "man": Nicodemus.

Nicodemus, John tells us, "came to Jesus by night" and believes in Jesus because he has seen him perform signs. "No one can do these signs that you do unless God is with him." Nicodemus clearly considers himself a disciple. He believes in Jesus. He's come to him to learn more. But again, for Jesus, it's not enough. There needs to be more: "Truly, truly I say to you, unless one is born of water and the Spirit, he cannot enter the kingdom of God" (Jn 3:2, 5).

As soon as that meeting is over, John makes clear, for anyone who doesn't understand, just what it means to be "born of water and the Spirit," telling us that, "After this Jesus and his disciples went into the land of Judea; there he remained with them and baptized" (Jn 3:22).

This pattern is repeated one more time in John 6. There, after Jesus has fed the multitudes with just a few loaves and fishes, the people come to him en masse, looking for more signs to help them believe and asking what they need to do to serve God: "What must we do to be doing the works of God.... What sign do you do, that we may see, and believe you?" (Jn 6:28, 30).

In reply, Jesus says, "I am the bread of life; he who comes to me shall not hunger, and he who believes in me shall never thirst" (Jn 6:35).

The reason those who come and believe will neither hunger and thirst is because they've been fed by the bread of life, Jesus, the Eucharist — they've been sacramentalized, given the power to be a disciple and live the life of faith.

Again and again, that's what John's Gospel drives home for us: the necessity of the sacraments. It reminds us that evangelization isn't a one-shot deal. It's not just the initial proclamation of the Gospel or the initial decision of belief. It's a lifelong process. It's a perpetual encounter with Christ understood through catechesis and accomplished through the sacraments.

~

That's what the first evangelists taught us: to proclaim Christ and proclaim him with word and deeds, to proclaim the Church, to proclaim the covenant to which we're called, and to proclaim the sacraments in which that covenant is forged and renewed. That's the Catholic Gospel.

It's a Gospel that reveals God as our loving Father, who established a covenant with us in the beginning, a covenant that we broke, leaving us in need of his mercy.

It's also a Gospel that tells us the solution to our sin came when God became man in Jesus Christ.

Jesus sealed the New Covenant with us through his self-sacrifice. He was then raised from the dead by the power of the Holy Spirit. Through the sacraments, in his Church, his resurrected life is conferred on us — and one day, by the mercy of God, that life will lead us to our true home: heaven.

All that was proclaimed in the old evangelization, and all of it must be proclaimed in the new.

The old evangelization, however, didn't end with the apostles. It began there. Afterward, countless men and women throughout the Roman Empire imitated and lived by the evangelists' message and methods. In their lives, in the lives of those early Christians, we find equally fundamental lessons for the New Evangelization.

.

# Chapter 7

~

# THE CATHOLIC LIFE:
# LESSONS FROM THE
# EARLY CHURCH

AMONG THE MANY TITLES CONFERRED ON ROME, one of the most apt is "the city of martyrs."

Long ago, the Christian faithful died for Jesus in her streets. Their blood soaked the ground of her arenas. Today, the churches that line those streets, and which stand where the arenas once stood, preserve their names for the ages.

The great apostles Peter and Paul, the virgins Agnes and Cecilia, the sisters Pudentiana and Praxedis — those saints and more bore witness to Christ through their deaths and played a pivotal role in the evangelization of the Roman world. For that, we built churches to honor them in the midst of the city where they died. We also celebrate them in the liturgy, and we write about them in history books.

But if we really want to understand the inner genius of that first evangelization — learning what lessons it might hold for the New Evangelization — it's not just to the great saints and martyrs of Rome that we need to look. We also need to look to the ordinary Christians — the men and women who bore witness to Christ through the normal routines of their daily lives. The history books that remember those men and women are few, and the churches that honor them almost nonexistent, but it may have been their witness, more than anything else, to which the old evangelization of the West owes its success.

## An Ancient War on Women

In his book, *The Rise of Christianity*, sociologist Rodney Stark paints a picture of what life in the ancient Roman Empire was like for women, both the rich and the poor. The picture is not a pleasant one.

To start with, many females didn't live longer than a day. That's because the Roman world saw daughters as a burden, not a blessing. With the complete sanction of the law, and for any reason whatsoever, fathers could murder or abandon their daughters within hours after their birth. Newborn sons faced a similar fate if they showed signs of physical deformity or weakness.

As the archaeological evidence attests, this patriarchal privilege wasn't just on the books. Inscriptions on the tombs in the ancient city of Delphi reveal that of the 600-plus families buried there, only six raised more than one daughter. In Rome, archaeologists have uncovered sewers literally clogged with the remains of newborns. And population records in Italy, Asia, and North Africa indicate that there were only 100 adult females for every 140 adult males.[23]

The commonplace nature of female infanticide comes across in this passage from a letter written by a husband, Hilarion, to his wife, Alis:

Know that I am still in Alexandria. And do not worry
if they all come back and I remain in Alexandria. I ask
and beg you to take good care of our baby son, and as
soon as I receive payment I shall send it up to you. If
you are delivered of a child [before I come home], if
it is a boy keep it, if a girl discard it.[24]

Even if a girl didn't have a father who thought her something to "discard," the life she grew into was rarely one any of
us would want for our daughters.

During the first ten to twelve years of her life, the average
Roman girl received little or no education. Then, somewhere
around the age of puberty (but often before), her father would
marry her off to a man much older than herself. The annals of
Roman history give us account after account of girls as young
as eleven or twelve marrying men aged fifty or older.[25]

After that, our typical Roman woman could look forward to a life where the law would never permit her to own
property, where it would, in fact, designate her as the property
of her husband (who could divorce her at a moment's notice
without cause). She could also look forward to sharing her
husband with a succession of mistresses and prostitutes — female or male — as well as undergoing one or more forced
abortions, abortions that were as likely to kill her as render
her infertile.

When the philosopher Thomas Hobbes described life as
"nasty, brutish and short," he almost perfectly summarized the
lives of women during the heyday of the Roman Empire.

## WOMEN'S LIBERATION

In contrast to that hellish female existence, the empire's Christian women fared far better.

Following the laws of the Jewish people, Christian communities strictly forbade both infanticide and abortion. Similar prohibitions existed against divorce, adultery, spousal abuse, and any form of unnatural relations. Husbands were urged to love their wives "as Christ loved the Church" (Eph 5:25), and Christian women had much greater freedom to take a husband or not as they saw fit.

While the average pagan women married at age twelve, most Christian women didn't marry until at least eighteen. If they were widowed, there was substantially less cultural pressure on them to remarry, and the Christian community helped see to their needs. As the years passed, Christians came to view virginity as the most noble of feminine vocations, and they encouraged women to serve the Church and study the Scriptures, giving them the freedom to run their lives with a degree of autonomy unheard of in pagan Rome.

All this was great news for early Christian women. But what did it mean for evangelization?

For one thing, it helped give Christians a demographic edge over their pagan counterparts.

During the first several centuries of Christianity, the population of Rome dramatically declined. No matter what rewards the emperors promised to families who bore at least three children (the minimum for population replacement), the population continued to shrink. With all the female infanticide, bad marriages, and abortions, it is little wonder that this was so.

But as pagan Rome died off, Christian Rome flourished. In part, that's because the Christians didn't kill their females. It's difficult to grow a population when you abandon female newborns and consign fertile young women to death from botched abortions.

Even more fundamentally, the Christian population grew because of the differences between how pagans and Christians viewed females and family life — differences that made Christianity vastly more attractive to women.

## MISSIONARY MARRIAGES

The historical data Stark highlights in his book shows that women made up a clear majority of the first Christian converts. In some communities, they seemingly outnumbered men by a four-to-one margin.[26]

From there, Stark reasons that as the number of pagan women continued to shrink and the number of Christian women continued to grow, pagan men increasingly had to go looking for wives in Christian communities. From that pool of pagan husbands, even more converts to Christianity were made.

The Christians' distinct attitude of respect toward women, however, as well as Christianity's recognition of the sacredness of family life, didn't affect only the demographics of evangelization.

As Catholics, we hear all the time that grace does not destroy or abolish human nature but instead presupposes it, builds upon it, and perfects it. And that's exactly the point that Stark arrives at in his book: that the Christian faith perfected marriage and relationships between the sexes, making for happier homes and more stable marriages.

Then, as now, that kind of happiness and stability was attractive. The ancient Romans saw in the home lives of the first Christians the kind of love, respect, and support for which they longed, for which we all were made. That intrigued them, attracted them, and eventually made new converts out of many of them.

From Stark's research, we can see how Christianity soon consumed city blocks and entire neighborhoods. It wasn't necessarily some extraordinary, miraculous, or ecstatic experience like the first Pentecost we read about in Acts 2; it was instead somewhat quiet, gradual, but substantive, and in some ways it brought about bigger and longer-lasting change.

That kind of evangelization didn't require great sacrifice or noble deeds. Rather, it required countless little sacrifices and daily deeds, all done in love. It required rejecting the cultural norms of the day — including infanticide, abortion, adultery, homosexuality, and the subjugation of women — and embracing a different way of life, a different way of seeing the human person.

What it required was a witness of life, not just of death, and although plenty of Christians stumbled and fell in their attempts to give that witness, they gave it nonetheless. And the culture took note.

## WORKS OF MERCY

The witness of life the early Christians gave, however, wasn't confined to their own homes. In their interactions with one another and with the larger community, they put their faith into practice.

Consider how the Christian community acted during the great plagues that swept the Roman Empire during the first few centuries after Christ.

In the ancient world, no war took as many lives as a mass epidemic. The ancients feared epidemics like we fear terrorism. More, probably. They didn't understand the causes, they rarely knew the cures, and — in the unimaginably crowded cities — they were incapable of stopping their spread.

Accordingly, when an epidemic struck, the wealthiest families fled to the country. The physicians fled right along with them. The rest of the people remained behind to die.

With no one to provide even the most basic nursing care, die they did. Parents abandoned sick children. Children abandoned sick parents. Neighbors abandoned neighbors. Family ties and friendships counted for nothing. Nor did the pagan faith. When the wealthy and the physicians fled, so did the priests from the temples. They had no consolation to offer the sick, no meaning to ascribe to their sufferings. They simply took their money and ran, while those who remained behind isolated themselves from one another, tossing the sickest out into the streets to die with those already dead.

In his book, Stark looks at two of the major epidemics that struck the Roman Empire — one in 165 and the other in 251 — and notes that each wiped out a quarter to a third of the empire's population. He also points out that those numbers didn't apply to the cities' Christian populations. Somehow, in the midst of all that dying, the Christians' numbers continued to grow.[27]

How was that possible?

Again, Christians didn't live like their pagan neighbors. Instead, they strove to live like Christ, which meant they stood ready to give their lives for one another. When others fled, Christians remained behind. They nursed their sick. They tended to their dying. They also tended to the pagan sick and dying — friends and neighbors abandoned by their families.

Writing in about the year 260, the Alexandrian Bishop Dionysius gives us this account of one of those mass epidemics:

> Most of our brother Christians showed unbounded love and loyalty, never sparing themselves and thinking only of one another. Heedless of danger, they took charge of the sick, attending their every need and ministering to them in Christ, and with them departed this life serenely happy; for they were in-

fected by others by a disease, drawing on themselves
the sickness of their neighbors and cheerfully accepting their pains … so that death in this form, the result
of great piety and strong faith, seems in every way the
equal of martyrdom.[28]

Other ancient accounts back up Dionysius' claims, including a letter from the great enemy of the Church, the emperor Julian, expressing his frustration with pagans who failed
to exercise the same great charity as the Christians.

"The impious Galileans support not only their poor but
our poor as well," he wrote in a letter to a friend. "Everyone
can see they lack aid from us."[29]

## COURAGEOUS LOVE

Everyone could indeed see, which is why Stark credits the
Christians' charity during these great epidemics as a major
factor in the growth of Christianity.

As with women and family, it was, in one way, a question of demographics. Even in the midst of horrible plagues,
basic nursing care reduces mortality rates by up to two-thirds.
Based on that, Stark projects that far fewer Christians died
from these epidemics. That in turn contributed to their relative growth rate in the cities.

Beyond survival rates, Christians' concern for one another
and their pagan neighbors was inspiring. To a world that believed suffering held no meaning, where the pagan faith could
offer neither comfort nor explanation for the tragedy unfolding and where basic kindness was in short supply, Christianity offered something entirely different. It offered meaning. It
offered comfort. And it offered a place in a community where
people would be loved and cared for, not deserted.

An ancient pagan once observed, "The stoics learned to overcome the fear of death by lifelong austere discipline, whereas the Christians overcome the fear of death by habit." That lack of fear is what pagan Rome saw in the Christians who nursed them, a lack of fear that not only exceeded that of the great stoics, but one marked, as Bishop Dionysius said, by a serene happiness.

Given all that, it's not surprising that many of the pagans who survived the plague converted to the religion of those who nursed them back to health. They wanted what the Christians had — serene happiness, not to mention joy, courage, community, and good health. In times of trial, the promises of the pagan world and the promises of Christ were both tested. One was found wanting.

## A People Set Apart

An early second-century document, *The Letter to Diognetus*, describes this process of cultural Christianization in subtle, yet profound terms.[30]

The letter begins by noting that "Christians are distinguished from others neither by country, nor language, nor the customs they observe."

To us, that might not seem all that striking an observation. But in the second century, that was radical stuff. As the Old Testament saw it, there were two races in the world — Jews and Gentiles. With the birth of the Church, it was as though a third race had come into being, a race of converted Jews and Gentiles who didn't distinguish themselves by country, language, or customs.

The letter continues:

In respect to clothing, food, and the rest of their ordinary conduct, they display to us their wonderful and extraordinary way of life.... They marry as do others, they beget children, but they do not commit infanticide. They have a common table, but not a common bed.... They obey the prescribed laws and at the same time, surpass the laws by their very lives. They love all men and are persecuted, practically, by all.... To sum it up, what the soul is to the body, so Christians are in the world.... The invisible soul is guarded by the visible body and Christians are known indeed to be in the world, but their Godliness remains largely invisible.

That's a remarkable passage, rich with lessons for the Church today. Three lines, however, stand out.

First, through "ordinary conduct, they display to us their wonderful and extraordinary way of life." Christians differentiated themselves from their contemporaries not primarily through facing the lions and going against the emperor but through ordinary conduct. In how they worked, how they loved their spouses and children, and how they cared for the poor, they lived as a people apart. The ancient world saw Christians going about the ordinary business of life in an extraordinary way and recognized it as such.

Second, "what the soul is to the body, so Christians are in the world." That describes the principle of animation, whereby our soul is dispersed through all the members of our body, enabling us to use our hands and eyes and voice to express our self, to express us. In a similar way, the author sees Christians scattered throughout society, animating it, giving life to it, and making the world more as God intended.

Finally, "their Godliness remains largely invisible." Invisibly, gradually, but inevitably and dramatically — that's how Christian faith, hope, love, doctrine, suffering, persecution, and fidelity transformed the pre-Christian pagan world. The

Gospel spread person to person, household to household, neighborhood to neighborhood, converting whole towns, then whole provinces, and finally the whole empire.

~

This is what St. Augustine meant when he described the process of conversion as one heart setting another heart on fire. And this is what can happen again today.

If that kind of ordinary witness could transform the pagan world, then we have no reason to believe it can't transform the post-Christian neo-pagan world in which we live. It succeeded against all odds back then, and if we apply the lessons learned from those who went before us, it can succeed against all odds once more.

But how do we start applying those lessons?

# Chapter 8

~

# The Primary Field of Evangelization: The Christian Family

Years ago, my wife, Kimberly, and I hosted a Sunday-night Bible study in our home. We would put the kids to bed and then spend the next two hours teaching, talking, and praying with the attendees, who were mostly students from the university where I teach. After a few years of this, my two oldest sons prevailed upon me to stay up and sit in on the Bible study. They were still young, but how does any dad answer no when his sons say, "Dad, we want to study the Bible too. Can we please stay up?"

One Sunday night, not long after I permitted them to start joining us, one young man took up quite a bit of time with some very technical questions about some obscure biblical passages. The boys took note of this, and after everyone else had left and we were cleaning up, they started imitating the questioner.

"Dr. Hahn," one said to me, "can you explain to us the theology of the vacuum cleaner."

"Dr. Hahn," said the other, "I'm really curious about the theological implications of this rug."

Seeing a looming problem behind the mocking, I cut them off right away.

"Hey, none of this 'Dr. Hahn' business," I said. "I'm 'Dad.' 'Doctor' is what I do, but 'Dad' is who I am."

That distinction is one I never wanted my boys to forget. The first is important: God has called me to a profession that allows me to serve him in many ways and many places. But before that, he's called me to a family. In that family, I give him my most important service. As a husband and father, I serve him in the most important ways. And how I serve him there affects how I serve him everywhere else.

The same holds true for each of us, married or single, parents or not parents: The family is where it starts. It's the primary field of evangelization, the primary place each one of us is called to proclaim Christ. And what we do there, in that innermost field of evangelization, radiates outward, affecting our work in every other field.

## The Domestic Church

Millennia ago, the witness of Christian families in the ordinary course of life made countless converts in pagan Rome. By showing "love in the little things" — in the way spouses cared for each other, tended their children, performed their daily work, and showed kindness to their neighbors — these families testified to the transforming power of grace and the beauty of the Christian life.

The efficacy of that particular form of witness was no coincidence. From the beginning, God intended the union of man and woman to be a sign, both of who he is and how he loves.

God, as John Paul II once explained, is not "a Solitude" but rather "a family," an eternal communion of love between the Father, the Son, and the Holy Spirit.[31] Through Baptism, we become part of that family, adopted children possessing God's own life — sanctifying grace — within us. We also become part of the Church, the bride of the Bridegroom, the beloved of the world's greatest Lover, who, as St. Paul tells us, gave himself up for his bride so that "she might be holy and without blemish" (Eph 5:25-27).

For those reasons and more, Paul could rightly call marriage a "profound" mystery (Eph 5:32). Through the union of man and woman, the fruitfulness of their love, the sacrifices they make because of their love, and the graces that come through those sacrifices, marriage "speaks" of God. It incarnates a reality too great for most of us to comprehend: God's faithful, fruitful, transforming love.

## THE WITNESS OF FAITHFUL LOVE

The fact that so many marriages today fall short of what God intended, ending in adultery or divorce or crippled by a contraceptive mind-set, doesn't lessen the efficacy of the sign. In fact, according to Pope Benedict XVI, it just makes the witness of those who do live in accordance with God's plan for marriage all the more powerful. He explains:

> The union of a man and a woman, their becoming "one flesh" in charity, in fruitful and indissoluble love, is a sign that speaks of God with a force and an eloquence which in our days has become greater because unfortunately, for various reasons, marriage … is going through a profound crisis.[32]

Noting the existence of "a clear link between the crisis in faith and the crisis in marriage," Benedict goes on to challenge Catholic couples not simply to let their marriages be transformed by the grace of faith but also to use their marriages as a means of communicating grace and truth to others. "As the Church has said and witnessed for a long time now," he concludes, "marriage is called to be not only an object but a subject of the new evangelization."

In that, Benedict issued a challenge to Catholics today similar to that issued by St. Augustine to Catholics of his day, when he addressed the fathers in his congregation as "my dear fellow bishops."[33]

Benedict understood in our time, as Augustine understood in his, that in order for the New Evangelization to succeed, Christians must recover a vision of the family as a domestic church. We must see our homes as places where the love of God is made visible and personal, where it is made real, and where the faith is handed on to future generations. We also must see our homes as special places of witness in the community, a sign in the midst of neighborhoods and businesses of the love to which God calls us.

The extent to which our families become faithful domestic churches is the extent to which both we and our children become capable of engaging in all the rest of the work of the New Evangelization. Whether God calls us to proclaim the Gospel in foreign lands or the house next door, we'll do both better for having cultivated a life of faith under our own roofs first.

And to do that, at least seven things are required.

## 1. Married couples must strive to live the vows made on their wedding day.

Putting an understanding of the domestic church into practice demands, first and foremost, the faithful love of the spouses.

"Husbands should love their wives as their own bodies" (Eph 5:28). Wives should do the same.

As husbands and wives, we are called to a holy vocation — sainthood — through a holy vocation — marriage. Our marriages are the context in which our ongoing conversion, our deepening of faith, takes place. And it's through dying to our self for the good of our spouse that we receive the grace we need for that conversion.

Practically speaking, that means we must be faithful. We must be kind. We must be attentive. We must bear with one another, forgiving each other as God forgives us (cf. 1 Cor 7:10-24; Eph 4:32). Above all, we must put our spouse first — before other relationships, other interests, other projects — recognizing through it all that God has called us to marriage not for the sake of our pleasure or comfort but rather for the sake of our sanctification, and that sanctification usually comes by way of daily deaths to self. Most of those deaths will be small — help offered generously, chores done promptly, complaints tempered, and thanks offered — but those small sacrifices help us receive the grace we need to take on bigger sacrifices when their time comes.

In the early Church, stable marriages graced by the sacraments and lived out through mutual support and respect helped make converts of millions. They can do the same today.

2. *Mothers and fathers must become the primary evangelizers of their children.*

In *Familiaris Consortio* (on the role of the Christian family in the modern world), Pope John Paul II notes that "parents are … the first heralds of the Gospel for their children," and that "the ministry of evangelization carried out by Christian parents is original and irreplaceable" (nn. 39 and 53).

That ministry isn't supposed to be an extraordinary one. It's supposed to be an ordinary part of parenting. Nor should we see parenting the children God gives us as a separate activity from evangelizing them. They're meant to be one and the same task.

The first lessons our children learn about God's love are learned from us. Not from what we read to them or explain to them but from how we love them. They learn to trust God when we are trustworthy. They learn that God will always be there for them if we are always there for them. They learn about God's strength and wisdom, mercy and justice, patience and kindness, when we are strong and wise, merciful and just, patient and kind. Or they don't. What they learn, in large part, will depend on us.

The same holds true for what they learn about the faith. Religion classes in schools or parishes can only help children learn so much. And they can't help children learn much at all if what's taught in school isn't reinforced at home.

Again, the primary responsibility for faith formation falls to parents, not to the parish priest or catechist. It's not enough for us to just faithfully love our spouse and love our faith. We also must actively work to form our children in the faith. It's our responsibility to proclaim Christ to them in word and deed, praying with them and talking to them about God — how he loves us, how he has shown that love in history, and how he continues to show it today. It's also our responsibility to get them to the sacraments as often as possible, to teach them how to show reverence for God both in and out of church, and to live lives of Christian charity. More than anyone else, it falls to parents, as the sage of Proverbs noted so long ago, to "Train up a child in the way he should go" (Prov 22:6a).

And if we do?

"When he is old he will not depart from it" (Prov 22:6b).

3. *Families must become places of prayer.*

When we look back at the writings of the early Church Fathers, we see that they're filled with accounts of families who took to heart Paul's words to "continue steadfastly in prayer, being watchful in it with thanksgiving" (Col 4:2). Some families, Tertullian tells us, structured their weeks around prayer through the observance of the stational prayers — specific fasts and prayers every Wednesday and Friday. Others rose at three in the morning simply to pray together.[34]

While I don't see a call to 3:00 a.m. prayer going over well in my house, that doesn't mean we can't imitate our forebears in the faith, being "constant in prayer" as a family (Rom 12:12). As families, we can pray the Rosary after dinner, say the Morning Offering together before everyone goes to school or work, or give our children a small blessing before putting them to bed at night. We can also recover lost Catholic traditions, like doing the enthronement of the Sacred Heart, building a small grotto in the backyard, setting up family altars in the living room, celebrating favorite saints' feast days with special dinners, abstaining from meat every Friday, and making the sign of the cross when passing a Catholic church. Each of those activities, some of which take only a few seconds of our time, present us with the opportunity to re-center our hearts and minds on God. They also help us teach our children that God is with us every moment of the day.

Children learn by imitation. That's true with language, and it's true with prayer. They learn to pray when we pray with them. They learn what it means to talk to God, when they hear us talk to God. They learn to go to God — in adoration, in thanksgiving, in contrition, and in supplication — when they see us go to God in those same ways.

Even more fundamentally, when we pray regularly as a family, we give God a greater opportunity to work with us, to give us the grace we need to face the challenges that await us and make the sacrifices the day asks of us. Bound together by grace, we become more capable of witnessing to Christ in the other fields to which he calls us.

Prayer really is the soul of our apostolate — or at least it should be. Whether at home or abroad, all our efforts for the New Evangelization need to be the overflow of our interior life. If they're not, the seeds we sow will have a much more limited yield.

### 4. The Mass must become the center of family life.

Again, if we look back on the witness of families during the first evangelization, we see that Christian families were intensely connected to the liturgical and devotional life of the Church.

In the year 304, in the North African city of Abitinia, Roman authorities arrested whole families for their Christian faith. When those families came before the judge, he offered them an easy out.

"All you have to do," he told them, "is not go to Mass on Sunday."

They didn't have to renounce Christ. They didn't have to stop loving their spouses or treating their neighbors with kindness. They just had to stop going to Mass. But that they would not do.

"We cannot live without the Mass," they told the judge.

And they never needed to. The judge promptly sent them to their deaths.[35]

For families in the world today, the choice should be much simpler. Going to Mass doesn't require that we choose between life and death. It just means choosing to prioritize God over our six-year-old's soccer game or the Sunday morning news shows. Those are the temptations we have to overcome in order to get to Mass at least every Sunday — and if possible, every day of the week.

And we do need to overcome them, for it's in the Mass that we give God the thanks and adoration he's due. And it's from the Mass, from Christ present in the Eucharist, that we receive the power to love as we're called to love. Everything else follows from that.

5.   *The domestic church must become a haven of charity.*

Again, in the early Church, the concern Christian families showed for others made pagan Rome sit up and take notice. As Tertullian explained it, "It is our care of the helpless, our practice of loving kindness that brands us in the eyes of many of our opponents who say, 'See those Christians — how they love one another.' "[36]

Those words of Tertullian's testify to the old saying: "Charity begins at home."

As families, how we speak to one another, the language we use, the tone of our voice, the respect our words and attitude convey, not to mention the affection we show in word and deed, is all a form of witness. It's a witness to our children, and it's a witness to our friends and neighbors.

The same holds true for striving to honor one another in all things. Believing the best of our family members and speaking the best of one another, prioritizing time with one another — not just to pray and teach but also to play, have fun, and really enjoy one another's company — is an ongoing testimony to the love and beauty of family life, as well as to the dignity of each person in the family.

While charity begins at home, though, it doesn't end there. The doors of our homes should always be open to those in need of company, conversation, or comfort. Christian hospitality, whether offered in the form of a dinner, a Bible study, or even a place to stay for those who need a home (for a little while or a long while) are all ways of taking the love we have for our family and letting it radiate outward.

So too are works of mercy, both corporal and spiritual. Visiting the sick, feeding the hungry, remembering the widows and the orphans — those acts should be as commonplace in our homes as Monday Night Football. More commonplace, actually.

The same applies to almsgiving. "Prayer with fasting is good," the Book of Tobit tells us, "but better than both is almsgiving with righteousness.... It is better to give alms than to lay up gold. For almsgiving saves from death and purges away every sin. Those who give alms will enjoy a full life" (Tob 12:8-9).

Note that when Jesus talks about almsgiving in Matthew 6:2 — "[W]hen you give alms, sound no trumpet before you" — he uses the word "when," not "if." For Jesus, there is no "if" about it. Almsgiving, as he sees it, is as essential to the Christian life as prayer itself. We need to see it the same way, heeding whenever possible the ancient tradition of tithing and giving generously to the work of the Church in our parish and around the world.

That practice — giving 10 percent of the first fruits of our labors — will seem challenging at first. Those who remain faithful to the practice, however, soon discover that God has a habit of returning tenfold what we give away. When it comes to generosity, he cannot be outdone.[37]

## 6. *We must be faithful.*

When you read the work of sociologists and historians such as Rodney Stark, one thing comes across loud and clear: the faithful were faithful. They believed what the Church taught, and they sought, above all else, to heed Christ's injunction to "observe all that I have commanded you" (Mt 28:20). That's why they were faithful to their spouses. That's why they didn't kill their infant girls or abort their children. That's why they cared for their dying neighbors. Because that's what the faith required of them. That's what it meant to be a Christian.

We need to follow suit, striving to live lives in accord with Church teaching and meeting the standard Christ set for us. It's a high standard. It doesn't just call us to reject what our sex-obsessed, modernist, materialist, consumer culture glorifies and glamorizes. It actually calls us to "be perfect" as our heavenly Father is perfect (Mt 5:48), overcoming the vices of vanity, pride, gluttony, greed, envy, lust, wrath, and sloth, while cultivating the virtues of detachment, humility, temperance, generosity, charity, chastity, patience, and fortitude.

That can seem impossible. And without grace, it would be. Even with grace, we'll often fall short. The early Christians certainly did. They struggled with temptation, stumbled, and fell. But then they repented. They confessed their sins, came back to the Church, and started all over again.

What they didn't do, however, was call a sin anything other than a sin. They didn't try to lower the Church's standards to the culture's level, calling abortion, infanticide, remarriage (without an annulment) after a divorce, homosexual acts, or contraception anything other than violations of God's law. The early Christians hated these sins as passionately as they loved the sinners who fell into them.

So must we.

### 7. *We must cultivate the virtue of hope.*

Every night, for more than thirty years now, my family has continued a tradition begun in my wife's family. Over dinner, every family member has to recall one good thing that happened to him or her that day. On Sunday, they have to recall one good thing that happened to them that week. We then write everyone's Sunday "good thing" down in a book we keep in the dining room.

There are days when it's easier to come up with "good things." There are days when it's harder. But it's always helpful. It cultivates a spirit of gratitude in Kimberly, me, and all the children. In effect, it helps us do what St. Paul told us to do in Philippians 4:8: "Finally, brethren, whatever is true, whatever is honorable, whatever is just, whatever is pure, whatever is lovely, whatever is gracious, if there is any excellence, if there is anything worthy of praise, think about these things."

Why does this matter? Well, as Stark points out, in the early Church there was a strong contrast between the despair that permeated the worldview of pagan Rome and the hope that Christians of that time possessed. The first Christians lived in hope. They rejoiced in it (Rom 5:2). They trusted in the promises of Christ. And they knew this world was not their home.

That hope gave them courage. "Since we have such a hope, we are very bold," wrote Paul (2 Cor 3:12). It also gave them freedom from the troubles that plagued the Roman Empire in its dying days. They felt free to love and practice generosity, to sacrifice themselves, and to bring life into the world, all because their hopes weren't bound up in this world. They were bound up in the next.

That hope brought new life to Western Civilization. It helped convert the population at a rate of 40 percent per decade for the first three centuries of Christianity, and it helped the faith endure even after the empire collapsed.[38]

We need to cultivate that same hope — in ourselves and in our families. We need to trust that for all the evil in our culture, all is not lost. Christ still reigns. We need to hold fast to him, do faithfully what he asks of us, and joyfully live the life the Church calls us to live.

Which brings me back to the "good things." For our family, that's what the "good things" tradition helps accomplish. It reminds us that there is reason to give thanks, reason to hope. It helps me as a father and Kimberly as a mother affirm our children and what's good in our lives. It helps us to provide the calm, trusting leadership that is essential to a happy home life and a happy spiritual life. In other homes, different traditions will accomplish the same. But in every home, Christians need to find a way to fight off anxiety and cultivate hope, because it is in that hope that we, like the early Christians, will find freedom. And as we do, our culture, too, can be transformed.

~

Christ calls each of us to discipleship — to follow him in all our comings and goings. He also calls each of us to be apostles — in Greek, *apostolos*, meaning, literally, one sent on a mission. For most of us, answering that call won't entail crossing oceans — more often, just streets. But we are sent nonetheless. We are on a mission, a mission that begins at home. And it falls to us to embark on that mission today, in this moment.

Some of us may wish that we had embarked on it earlier, that we had learned about this mission when we were younger or when our children were younger. But there's no going back. We can't change what's past. We can only change what we do here and now. And it is never too late to say yes to this mission. It's never too late to begin the work of the New Evangelization in our marriages and homes. Whatever we give God now and in the days ahead, he will use it to bear great fruit.

It's also important to remember that these truths apply just as much to single people as they do to married people. God calls all men and women to spiritual fatherhood and spiritual motherhood. He calls all of us to a faithful spousal relationship with him in eternity. He calls all of us to place the Eucharist at the center of our lives, to make our homes havens of charity and hospitality, and to cultivate a prayerful, hopeful, and faithful spirit.[39]

Single people may answer those calls differently than married people — through their relationships with parents, siblings, godchildren, and roommates, rather than with spouses and children — but they're called to answer them just the same. On their answer, as much as on that of married couples, the success of the New Evangelization will hinge.

That answer, however, isn't only given in the home. It's also given in the world.

# Chapter 9

~

# FARTHER AFIELD:
# THE LAY APOSTOLATE

THE FAMILY IS WHERE IT ALL STARTS. It is, in a sense, the epicenter of the New Evangelization. Husbands and wives, sons and daughters, brothers and sisters — all of us are called to pattern our lives on the inner life of God. We're called to live lives of radical fidelity, charity, and self-gift within the four walls of our home.

But those lives of radical fidelity, charity, and self-gift don't end there. They start there, empowering us to live those lives farther afield.

That call came through loud and clear at the Second Vatican Council in the conciliar document *Apostolicam Actuositatem*. Something of a Magna Carta for the lay apostolate, the document lays out the Church's marching orders for the baptized but unordained, calling the laity to a life of apostolate in the world.

Note that word: apostolate. Not ministry. The difference is significant.

## SALT AND LIGHT

When I entered the Church in 1986, I thought I knew the Catholic faith. And I did. I knew the theology. I knew the doctrines. I knew the history. But, as I soon discovered, that was the easy stuff to learn. Much harder were the little things — the habits of custom and life that came so instinctively to people raised in the Church but which felt foreign to a former Protestant like me.

This was particularly true when it came to language, of how I spoke about the faith. It took years to break old habits of speech and acquire new ones — for example, referring to Jesus as "Our Lord," not "the Lord"; speaking of "evangelization," not "evangelism"; the "homily," not the "sermon"; or Mary as "the Blessed Mother" or "Our Lady." It also took me a while to learn to make the distinction between "ministry" and "apostolate."

What's the difference?

Ministry, literally, means "the work of religious ministers." It is, primarily, what the clergy do. It's the privileged term for the administration of the sacraments by those duly ordained. It doesn't exclude lay people, but it nevertheless remains the work proper to bishops, priests, and deacons.

Apostolate, on the other hand, is defined as "the work of the apostles." It's the work of all those called and sent by Christ. That's why *Apostolicam Actuositatem* always uses the word "apostolate," never "ministry," to talk about the laity's mission in the world. It recognizes the different calls and the different fields to which those calls take us.

To confuse the two words and speak of the "ministry" of the laity isn't just a problem of semantics. Rather, it reveals a subtle form of clericalism that can undermine the lay mission.

Once, in the years before Vatican II, clericalism manifested itself as the dictum to "Pay, pray, and obey." It reflected a kind of ecclesial paternalism, where the parents encouraged the kids not to grow up by promising to always take care of them. It was a counterfeit paternity — true fatherhood requires raising sons and daughters who can become adults in their own right. But many of the Church's sons and daughters went along with it nonetheless, choosing not to study the Bible or develop a mature, well-informed faith.

After Vatican II, clericalism didn't go away. It just took on a different form. Instead of heeding *Apostolicam Actuositatem*'s call to become salt and light in the culture, many lay people came to believe that living their faith meant taking on a liturgical role during the Mass. They became extraordinary ministers of Holy Communion or lectors, and advocated for more roles for the laity in the Church's liturgy.

At the same time, plenty of priests did just the opposite, thinking that engaging the culture meant shedding their clerical garb and relinquishing liturgical duties to the laity.

Both the clergy and the laity turned the Church's vision for engagement with the culture on its head, failing to see that in the Body of Christ, each member has his or her proper tasks.

As St. Paul explains:

For the body does not consist of one member but of many. If the foot should say, "Because I am not a hand, I do not belong to the body," that would not make it any less a part of the body. And if the ear should say, "Because I am not an eye, I do not belong to the body," that would not make it any less a part of the body. If the whole body were an eye, where would be the hearing? If the whole body were an ear, where would be the sense of smell? But as it is, God arranged the organs in the body, each one of them, as he chose. If all were a single organ, where would the

body be? As it is, there are many parts, yet one body.
(1 Cor 12:14-20)

It no more serves to have everyone striving to do the
work of the ordained than it serves to have every member of
our body — hands, eyes, and elbows — trying to do the work
of the feet. The ordained have their tasks. We, the laity, have
ours. We're called to develop an apostolate in the world, to go
out into the many fields spread before us, and there both sow
and cultivate the seeds of faith.

So, to what other fields besides marriage and family must
we go?

## FRIENDSHIP

According to the ancient Greeks, a friend isn't just someone with whom we enjoy watching the game or having a
drink. Rather, they thought of a friend as a brother or sister,
a kinsman by affection rather than blood. They also spoke of
a friend as "another self," someone with whom you were so
closely bound that his joys and sorrows became your joys and
sorrows.

The ancient Israelites viewed things in a similar light. "A
faithful friend is a sturdy shelter," the Book of Sirach tells us.
"He that has found one has found a treasure" (Sir 6:14).

As Christians, that understanding of friendship should
shape our own. In an age where we use the term "friend" to
describe hundreds of strangers on Facebook, many of whom
we've never met, it's easy to be casual about friendship, to not
take its blessings or its responsibilities seriously. But friendships, when rightly valued and fostered, can be just as important as family. And when it comes to evangelization, friendship
can be almost as fundamental a field of endeavor as the family.

In many ways, the same methods we use for witnessing to the faith in our homes apply to how we witness to the faith among our friends. Whether those friends are Catholics or atheists, devout or lukewarm, the way we listen to them, speak to them, encourage them, support them, help them, and honor them all says something to them about the faith.

If we're a good friend — loyal and true — we give a positive witness. If we're not a good friend — if we're selfish and self-absorbed — then our witness is much less fruitful. "A sinful man will disturb friends and inject enmity among those who are at peace" (Sir 28:9).

Friendship, like family, is another form of shared life. And to take on the work to which we're called in this particular field — to help those who are searching and questioning — is to share our life in Christ with our friends.

That means inviting friends to share in our home life — birthdays and movie nights, holiday celebrations and the evening Rosary. It also means sharing with them the blessings and graces that have come to us by way of our faith — our joy, our wisdom, our peace.

It may mean challenging our friends when they wander on to the wrong path — holding them accountable when they behave badly at work or in their personal relationships — and allowing ourselves to be held accountable and to be challenged when we behave badly. It may mean offering to help out with the grocery bill when a friend unexpectedly loses a job, and accepting the same help when the situation is reversed. It most definitely means talking with them about Christ — sharing freely with them what he's doing in our life or what we're learning about him in the Scriptures, perhaps inviting them to join us at Mass or a Bible study, exchanging books and answering questions as they arise.

Along with all that, it means interceding for them — asking them how we can pray for them and then following through with our promise to take their needs to Our Lord in prayer. If it feels appropriate, we can even invite them to join us in prayer right then. A well-timed "Let's just say a quick prayer about that right now" can often elicit the most surprising results: tears, joy, peace, and thanksgiving. We can't always make that suggestion — with certain people or in certain times and places, it won't be appropriate — but we can and should make it more often than we do.

Friendship, in fact, provides a sheltering place for many people as they explore the implications of belief and a life of faith. We can offer that shelter, support, and encouragement remembering that no matter what we do, the journey from unbelief to belief can be a long one. In *Forming Intentional Disciples,* Sherry Weddell does an excellent job of documenting the key steps most adults take when they are on the journey to faith. It's a journey that starts with trust (in a person, an institution, a book), moves on to curiosity about Christ and his Church, and manifests next in openness to belief. It then moves on to seriously hungering and seeking a relationship with Christ and knowledge of his Church, before finally culminating in a commitment to discipleship.

Those are the stages of most every journey, but how an individual moves through them, how long it takes to move from one stage to the next, is a singular thing. As a friend, we need to respect that process. We can't rush or force anyone's journey. But we can walk with the person, offering whatever advice or guidance or prayers they need along the way.[40]

In the end, the important thing to remember is that evangelizing friends who don't share our faith doesn't mean beating them over the head with our Bibles. Kindness and loyalty are often the most effective witness. But we also can't hide our faith from them. We can't sequester it from our relationship any more than we can sequester it from our spouse or our children. Our faith is part of who we are, and if we want to lead our friends either to faith or to a deeper faith, it has to be integrated in word and deed into our relationships with them.

## THE NEIGHBORHOOD

Just as our concept of friendship has been watered down by social media, the traditional neighborhood has also suffered a hit from our post-modern way of life. In cities and suburbs alike, people live alongside one another without knowing one another. Families have back decks, not front porches, while barred doors and windows, tall backyard fences, four-car garages, and spacious yards all work in combination with our own busy schedules to keep us apart.

Nevertheless, the old injunction still holds: "You shall love your neighbor as yourself" (Mt 19:19). In part that requires that we, like those Roman Christians in days gone by, proclaim the faith by a life of witness on the streets where we live. Our family may be the only Catholic family the bachelor across the street or the lesbian couple next door ever meets, which makes our witness in our neighborhoods singular for them.

As for how we live that witness, it starts with the little things: exercising good stewardship of our homes and yards by keeping them neat and in good repair; letting our neighbors see us play with our children, support our spouse, and enjoy our families; smiling and waving at those we encounter as we walk the dog or head out for our evening run. All those things may seem insignificant or tangential to the faith, but in strangers' eyes, they're not. They're indicators of whether or not we walk the talk. They're testimonials to the order, beauty, and joy the faith brings to our life.

Beyond that, it falls to us to reach out and build community within our neighborhoods. We do that by getting to know our neighbors — introducing ourselves, inviting families over for barbecues or a drink on the deck, or maybe even organizing a neighborhood block party.

Acts of service also figure into the equation. We may not have to tend to neighbors dying from mysterious plagues, but making a meal for a family with a new baby or a widow grieving the loss of her husband still makes the love of Christ concrete. So too does sending a son over to mow the single neighbor's lawn, paying a Sunday-afternoon visit to the elderly couple up the block, or planning a neighborhood-wide cleanup day. And, as with our friends, we can ask our neighbors how we can pray for them — then, if the moment is right, invite them to pray with us then and there.

Through all those encounters, people see our faith at work. They get the chance to know us — to come to understand what motivates us and inspires us. They also have the opportunity to ask questions about our faith, and we have the opportunity to more freely share it. Ultimately, prejudices break down, lines of communication open, and community begins to grow. That, more often than not, is when conversion happens.

We need to remember that what draws most people to the Church or inspires them to grow deeper in their faith isn't Catholicism as an abstract idea. Rather, it's Catholicism as a way of life. It's seeing the faith lived out in a family or a community. That's what initially attracts someone or leads them to question their own life and beliefs.

That's not to say that we can't canvass our neighborhood (going door-to-door to share our faith), drop off a CD about Catholicism, or invite people to RCIA. We can, and often we should. Building community in our neighborhoods and door-to-door evangelization aren't mutually exclusive undertakings. But the fruits of the latter will be that much greater if it's not the doors of strangers on which we knock, but rather the doors of friends.

## At Work

In the United States, we spend a great deal of time focusing on "what" we do. We plan our education and often our lives around it, knowing that the titles we accumulate on our résumé will, in large part, determine how society sees us.

But as Catholics seeking to serve as missionaries in the marketplace, we have to learn to see things differently. For us, it shouldn't be as much about what we do, as how we do it. In other words, the most important thing about our professional life isn't whether we're doctors, lawyers, or heavy-machinery operators. It's whether we're good employees and good friends on the job, paying heed to Paul's instructions in the Letter to the Colossians: "Whatever your task, work heartily, as serving the Lord and not men" (Col 3:23).

To put that advice into action, we need to do our job well — working hard, using our time responsibly, paying attention to details, and following through on what we say we'll do. "In all your work be industrious" (Sir 31:22). We also need to deal honestly with others and God, making sure that nothing we do on the job in any way goes against our beliefs as Catholics or harms human dignity. In essence, we need to keep our work life and our faith life integrated, not compartmentalized, so that every aspect of our life can be a gift of service to God.

Tending this field, however, requires that we be more than good workers. It also requires we be good co-workers or employers.

Whether we're the person whose name is on the letterhead or the person who delivers the mail, we need to treat all those with whom we work with kindness and respect. That means praising someone for a job well done and showing interest in them as a person, not just as a worker — remembering birthdays, celebrating the birth of a child, and just taking the time to ask about their kids or parents or the marathon they ran over the weekend. It also means occasionally offering to pick up some extra work so a co-worker can stay home with a sick child, saying "please" and "thank you" for even the most mundane requests, and just smiling and saying "good morning" like we mean it at the beginning of the day.

If we want to share the Gospel with the people we see Monday through Friday, we can't be one person at work and another person at home or at Church on Sunday. We may not have the time to engage in lengthy conversations about the *Summa*. We may not have the freedom to hang pictures of the Sacred Heart on our office door. But we can live an integrated life that reflects what we believe. We can offer those with whom we work a constant example of how faith transforms a life and sustains it even in the midst of sorrows and stress. We can be a friend for the lonely and a reminder for the confused that there's more to life than money, sex, or power.

From there, we can do more. We can start a Bible study during lunchtime and ask co-workers to join us. We can tell the fallen-away Catholic in the office next door that we're stopping by a nearby parish after work to pray, and ask if she would like to come with us before grabbing a drink. We can invite friends from the office over for dinner with our family, to an apologetics talk at our parish, or Mass and brunch on Sunday. Even just mentioning that we're going to confession on our way home from work can serve as a gentle reminder to those who've been away from the sacraments for too long.

We can likewise heed St. Peter's advice: "Always be prepared to make a defense to any one who calls you to account for the hope that is in you," (1 Pet 3:15). We do that by speaking up and defending the Church when she's attacked in conversations we have on the job, choosing not to let the fear of standing out silence us. In that, we can become a source of accurate information about the faith (and maybe good reading material) where there wouldn't otherwise be one.

We also do that by being able to give a succinct account of our own conversion, reversion, or experience of faith. Protestants are often trained to give a three- or five-minute version of what they call their "testimony" — how they came to know Jesus as their Lord and Savior. It can strike some Catholics as odd, but it's actually a tremendously successful tool for evangelization. It personalizes the faith and makes it more real by making it concrete in one person's life. It also makes the teller more human, putting flesh on our own hopes and struggles. Catholics should be able to do something similar — not so we can walk up to strangers on the street or into random co-workers' offices and share our story unannounced (that's rarely effective), but so that, if someone asks us why we believe or how we can be so certain about the Church, we have a ready answer at hand.

Whatever we do, we shouldn't necessarily expect to see results right away. Our task, when it comes to evangelization in the places we work, is to plant seeds and do what we can to cultivate an office culture where faith and charity can flourish. Maybe we'll see the fruit those seeds bring forth. Maybe we won't. But we sow them nonetheless.

## THE PARISH

As in the family, the father — the pastor — is the head of the parish. He ultimately bears the responsibility for what the parish does and the direction it takes. But without his parishioners' help — their gifts and talents, expertise, and time — leading his parish in the right direction would be impossible. The most vibrant, faithful, effective parishes are always built on the partnership of priest and laity, with the pastor providing strong, faithful guidance that facilitates a mature and active faith in the congregation.

How do we cultivate that partnership?

First, through our active participation in the liturgy. That active participation doesn't entail taking on a liturgical role. We don't have to distribute Communion or read from the lectern to participate in the Mass. But we do have to engage our hearts, minds, and bodies in the mysteries unfolding before us. We have to fully enter into the Mass, offering our own lives on the altar where Christ offers his. We have to seek greater understanding of what the Mass is and what Christ accomplishes through it. The more we understand that, the more profoundly his graces can touch us and transform us, equipping us for our mission in the world.

Beyond the liturgy, the Church also entrusts to the laity the task of helping the parish carry out its mission to lead people to Christ. How each of us does that will differ according to gifts, talents, and our state in life, but there are no shortages of ways. "Having gifts that differ according to the grace given to us, let us use them" (Rom 12:6) — volunteering at our parish's food pantry, singing in the Church choir, coaching soccer at the parish school, visiting shut-ins, serving on the parish finance council, taking on a weekly Holy Hour, or just going to Mass twenty minutes early to pray the Rosary with others.

If none of those programs or devotional groups exists in our parish, we can talk to the priest about starting them ourselves. We don't have to wait for the pastor to launch a support group for grieving widows or put together a fellowship for new moms. With his permission, we can do those things ourselves. We can also organize prayer groups and Bible studies, parish missions, and service projects in our communities. We can bring in speakers, host movie nights for families, and dances for teens.

We can also orient our gaze outward, putting together teams to go door-to-door and invite baptized Catholics living within the parish boundaries back to Mass. That initiative not only benefits the people who take us up on the invitation; it benefits those issuing the invitation, with the evangelizers becoming the evangelized as they share the faith with others.

Whatever we do, in order for the New Evangelization to succeed, we can't think of our parishes as the equivalent of spiritual gas stations — places where we go once a week to fill up on sacramental graces, then forget about until the tank starts running low. Our parishes need to be our spiritual homes, our spiritual families. They're where we're fed, yes. But they're also where we help feed others. Our contributions, however small they may be, are essential. And, as with so many things in life, the more we contribute, the more we receive.

## "THE BACK FORTY"

All Catholics are called to witness to the faith among our family and friends, as well as in our neighborhoods, workplaces, and parishes. For the laity, those are the universal fields of the New Evangelization. But they're not the only fields. There are others, which, although not universal, are still essential. And it falls to each of us to discern if God is calling us to those fields, as well as what he's calling us to do there.

Those fields are at least four in number.

### 1. University Campuses

For Catholic parents, sending a child off to college is a frightening moment. And rightly so. Statistics tell us that 85 percent of the young people who are confirmed will leave the Church within the next fifteen years. Most of them will leave the Church in college, where 70 percent of the students who enter practicing their faith leave not practicing their faith.[41]

Unfortunately, it's not hard to understand the reasons behind those statistics. Given the catechetical breakdown in many homes, schools, and parishes, few young people now leave home with a mature, well-formed faith. When the support system that encouraged them to practice their faith — the family or a parish youth group — is gone, they make easy prey for all the temptations to unbelief and sin that come their way on college campuses.

There are, of course, colleges where this doesn't happen, colleges that support and equip students to know and live their faith (I happen to teach at one of these colleges). Those schools are the exception, however, not the rule. At most schools, something more is needed so that "we may present every man mature in Christ" (Col 1:28).

Right now, that "more" is taking the shape of campus-ministry groups, like the outstanding Newman Center at the University of Illinois (Champaign/Urbana) and the Fellowship of Catholic University Students (FOCUS).

FOCUS is particularly remarkable, having grown exponentially since its founding a little more than a decade ago. The Denver-based apostolate now has more than four hundred missionaries serving on seventy-four college and university campuses. Through Bible studies, prayer meetings, large group outreach, and one-on-one mentoring, FOCUS missionaries help some students find faith and others deepen their faith. In many ways, FOCUS is *the* model for how the New Evangelization needs to unfold on college campuses, and over the next decade the demand for FOCUS missionaries — and Catholic laity willing to support and sponsor those missionaries — will only grow.

### 2. The Media

Throughout his pontificate, Pope Benedict XVI called Catholics to take up the tools of social media and use them to engage the culture. He understood that the media is a powerful tool for communicating ideas, telling stories, and influencing humanity. He also understood that it's a tool often wielded poorly and for bad ends, with both Catholics and the truth shut out of the mainstream press.

The advent of social media, however, combined with the growing reach of new and alternative media, has changed the playing field. Catholics now have more tools than ever before to tell our story and proclaim the Gospel — which is why both supporting and using those tools is critical.

EWTN, Catholic radio, and Catholic newspapers such as *Our Sunday Visitor* and the *National Catholic Register* do much of the heavy lifting when it comes to responsible coverage of political and cultural events from a Catholic perspective. St. Joseph Communications and Lighthouse Media get the best Catholic speakers on CD and into homes and parishes. Groups such as Catholics United for the Faith, Word on Fire Ministries, Catholic Answers, and my own St. Paul Center for Biblical Theology also use the new media to disseminate Bible studies, apologetics courses, and commentary on all things Catholic. Then there are blogs such as CatholicVote.org and the Patheos Catholic portal, as well as thousands of personal blogs, Twitter feeds, and even Facebook — all used by Catholics to proclaim truth in the culture.

God doesn't call everyone to write a blog or host a Catholic radio show. But through taking advantage of the information and formation those outlets offer, as well as using our own Facebook pages or Twitter accounts to witness to the faith, we contribute to the New Evangelization, enabling "the infinite richness of the Gospel to find forms of expression capable of reaching the minds and hearts of all."[42]

### 3. Conferences and Retreats

Like the media, Catholic conferences are both a field and a tool. They're a field, where people come to be evangelized, and they're a tool to evangelize those who come. Importantly, they're also a proven tool, one that has been leading people to conversion, ongoing or otherwise, long before many of the apostolates in existence today were doing the work of the New Evangelization. As such, they're likely to continue to play an important role for years to come.

As for what makes for a successful Catholic conference, Franciscan University's Summer Conferences, which began in the mid-1970s, helped establish the model for that. Typically, it's a combination of inspirational or formational talks, time for prayer and fellowship, opportunities for confession, and the Holy Sacrifice of the Mass. Franciscan's success has led countless parishes, dioceses, and apostolates to adapt the model to suit their own needs, with men's conferences, women's conferences, and apologetics conferences now a standard component of Catholic formation in the United States.

The same model is increasingly being adapted for Europe, and over the last several years family conferences, "theology of the body" conferences, and pro-life conferences have taken place for the first time in many parts of Western Europe. Whether they bear the same fruit there that they've borne in the United States is yet to be seen.

Regardless of where we live, however, retreats, too, are an important component of the New Evangelization and shouldn't be underestimated. Whether they're personal retreats or guided retreats, these times of quiet and reflection have long played an instrumental role in individuals hearing the still, quiet voice of God, then allowing him to lead them to a place of deeper trust and belief. Not too long ago, retreats were considered so instrumental to the life of faith that, at schools like Marquette University, every undergraduate was required to make a personal retreat annually.

Over the past fifty years, that practice has ceased. Now, only a relative handful of the most committed Catholics make a habit of an annual or semi-annual retreat. A recovery of this practice, as well as greater encouragement to consider it, would bear great fruits for the Church in general and the New Evangelization in particular.

### 4. The New Lay Movements

Although they have been more of a force in Europe than in the United States, movements such as Focolare, Communion and Liberation, and the Neocatechumenal Way have helped millions of Catholics better understand and live the Catholic life. Other groups — such as the Militia Immaculata, the Apostolate for Family Consecration, and the Legion of Mary — have done the same.[43]

In many countries, these groups have sprung up where parishes were weak and opportunities for faith formation few. In other countries, they've complemented, rather than supplemented, parish life. In both cases, they offer Catholics a unique but equally valid form of Catholic spirituality that helps them better live their faith in the world. John Paul II, who convened many of these groups at an international lay-movement congress in 1998, saw their existence as a sign of a new springtime of the faith and of the "outpouring of the Holy Spirit." He encouraged the groups in their work, explaining:

> In our world, often dominated by a secularized culture which encourages and promotes models of life without God, the faith of many is sorely tested, and is frequently stifled and dies. Thus we see an urgent need for powerful proclamation and solid, in-depth Christian formation. There is so much need today for mature Christian personalities, conscious of their baptismal identity, of their vocation and mission in the Church and in the world! There is great need

for living Christian communities! And here are the
movements and the new ecclesial communities: they
are the response, given by the Holy Spirit, to this critical challenge at the end of the millennium. You are
this providential response.[44]

As we move ahead with the work of the New Evangelization, through our support, participation, or cooperation with
these groups, we recognize the same.

~

"The harvest is plentiful, but the laborers are few" (Mt 9:37).
Those words were true two thousand years ago, and they're
true today. There is no shortage of men and women who need
to hear what Christ has to say. There is no shortage of men
and women who need Christ. But there is a shortage of laborers. There is a shortage of Catholics willing to live their faith
with radical fidelity, boldly and beautifully, in the many fields
of the New Evangelization.

Christ, through his Church, calls you and me to change
that. He calls us to give our lives to the work of sowing seeds
for him.

Answering that call, however, requires more than a willing
heart. It also requires a mind formed by the truths we proclaim. And that brings us to the last piece of the puzzle: the
substance of the Catholic Gospel.

# PART III

~

# THE MESSAGE:
# THE CONTENT OF THE
# NEW EVANGELIZATION

# Chapter 10

~

# FALLEN FROM GRACE:
# THE NATURE OF SIN

IT TAKES EXACTLY TEN SECONDS TO PROCLAIM THE GOSPEL.

In a mere one-sixth of a minute, you can pronounce the four basic pillars of the faith: (1) God loves you; (2) we have sinned; (3) Christ has died for our sins and risen from the dead; and (4) we have to respond to those gifts by faith.

It takes a whole lot longer, however, to understand those four truths and let them transform how we see the world and live within it.

That transformation is the heart of the New Evangelization. It's what a life of ongoing conversion — of falling ever more deeply in love with God — is all about. It's also the goal, both for ourselves and for those we seek to reach.

God's grace will get us to that goal. Only grace can make that transformation possible. But we participate in the process through the use of our intellect and will. It falls to us to strive to know what we proclaim as Catholics, and it falls to us to cooperate with the grace God gives us to live by these truths. It falls to us to strive to grasp the depths of the Gospel.

That's why, in this last section of the book, we're going to put flesh on the *kerygma*, examining the content of the New Evangelization — the message Christ calls us to proclaim.

And we're going to start with us — with who we are and how far we've fallen.

## In the Garden

In the opening chapter of Genesis, God reveals to us that we are his creatures, his creations, made "in his own image" (Gen 1:27). Genesis 2 then recounts how God created us: from the dust. Yet in the same sentence that reveals our humble origins, we also encounter something remarkable: "The Lord God formed man of dust from the ground, and breathed into his nostrils the breath of life; and man became a living being" (Gen 2:7; RSV).

The word for "living being" used there is *nephesh*, which could be translated as "soul." It's more than that, though, because that line suggests the first breath man draws is more than oxygen. It's more than the air the other creatures — the horses, dogs, cows, and cats — breathed. It's the breath of God, the Spirit of God. It's the grace of divine adoption whereby a lofty creature made with free will and human reason is elevated to share in the grace of divine life. That breath made man not just the ruler of creation but also God's child, his by grace.

What this means for us is that there is life and there is *life*. There is the life that is human and natural to us, and there is the life that is supernatural and divine.

When we understand that, we can also understand God's warning to Adam and Eve in the subsequent verses: "And the Lord God commanded the man, saying, 'You may freely eat of every tree of the garden; but of the tree of the knowledge of good and evil you shall not eat, for in the day that you eat of it you shall die' " (Gen 2:16-17).

In Hebrew, the word for death is doubly stressed. The literal translation there is "you shall die the death."

If we don't understand that there is more than one type of life to lose, that warning, let alone the emphasis placed on the word "death," makes no sense. After all, once Eve and then Adam listen to the serpent and disobey God, nothing seemingly happens. They don't keel over on the spot. By all appearances, they're as strong and healthy as they were before taking a bite of the forbidden fruit.

But again, there is life and there is *life*. If the serpent had bitten Adam, he might have keeled over and died. He might have lost his natural life. His supernatural life, however, his life as God's adopted son, would have remained as vibrant as ever.

As it was, the serpent didn't bite Adam. But Adam did disobey God. He committed a mortal sin — "a sin unto death" (1 Jn 5:16) — using his free will to go against God's will. That cost him the far more precious life within his soul. It wasn't less of a death. It was infinitely more of a death. He forfeited his divine sonship. He forfeited sanctifying grace.

## OUR INHERITANCE

For their disobedience, Adam and Eve paid a heavy price. God cast them out of Eden, bereft of sanctifying grace. Eventually, they lost their natural lives as well, but not before handing on their impoverished human nature to their children, who, in turn, passed the same down to us.

That impoverishment is what Catholics allude to when talking about original sin.

The fifth session of the Council of Trent, which met in 1546, gives us one of my favorite definitions of original sin:

> Adam, when he had transgressed the commandment of God in Paradise, immediately lost the holiness and justice wherein he had been constituted ... he incurred, through the offense of that prevarication, the wrath and indignation of God, and consequently death, with which God had previously threatened him, and together with death captivity under his power who thenceforth had the empire of death, that is to say the Devil....[45]

This definition from Trent is significant because it helps us understand the difference between Protestant and Catholic conceptions of original sin.

In the reformed Protestant world, original sin is understood not only as the consequence of Adam's sin; it's also understood as the guilt we incur. Historically, the Protestant view is one of total depravity. We inherit original sin from our first parents, and their guilt is imputed to us on account of their transgression. We stand accused and convicted from the start.

As Catholics, however, we believe that original sin isn't something committed; it's something contracted. We recognize that we have received from Adam and Eve a human nature devoid of the divine nature God originally entrusted to them. As such, we don't so much see original sin as a "thing," as we do a lack of a "thing" — that "thing" being sanctifying grace. And sanctifying grace isn't just religious rhetoric for something special. It is the Holy Trinity dwelling within the soul.

What that means for us is that we receive a human nature from the moment of our conception. But because we receive a human nature without a divine nature, we're spiritually dead from the start. That's our inheritance from our first parents: spiritual death. We're physically alive but spiritually dead because the life of God does not dwell within us.

Baptism, however, changes that.

Sometimes, we talk about Baptism as "wiping away the stain of original sin." But that's a flawed metaphor. It inadvertently suggests that something is there before Baptism that isn't there afterward — almost as if we could perform a spiritual x-ray of our soul, both before and after Baptism, showing first a dirty soul, which is later made shiny and new. But again, it's not the presence of something before Baptism that's the problem. It's the absence, the absence of divine life.

That divine life is what Baptism restores. It gives us back the divine life that Adam and Eve lost.

## OUR CONTRIBUTION

Even after Baptism, however, not everything is as it was. There's still this little problem known as concupiscence.

Concupiscence refers to our human appetites or desires, which remain disordered due to the temporal consequences of original sin. In and of itself, concupiscence isn't a sin; it's the result of original sin. It's also the cause of actual sin.

Again, this is a crucial distinction from how most Protestants understand concupiscence. For them, not only is original sin something that renders you guilty and inherently deserving of hell forever, but concupiscence (at least for Luther) is just as bad as actual sin. Consequently, no matter what you try to do right for God, no matter what temptations you resist, you're still just a dirty worm, someone whose "righteous deeds are like filthy rags" (Is 64:6). In Luther's mind, the best things we do are still sins.

Not so, according to the Catholic Church. Instead, the Church recognizes that like original sin, concupiscence is something we've contracted, not committed. As the Church sees it, original sin does to our soul something akin to what a tornado does to a landscape or what a two-year-old does to a toy room. It disrupts the order of things, so even when Baptism restores the divine life to our soul, disorder remains.

That disorder is concupiscence. It consists of a darkened intellect, a weakened will, and disordered affections and appetites. The intellect can still know the truth, but it has a harder time discovering the higher truths. They're no longer self-evident, as they were to our first parents — nor, to the concupiscent mind, is perceiving those truths wholly desirable.

The same holds true for the will. Even when the intellect presents the will with the highest truths, the will itself recoils or rebels against them. Why? Because concupiscence is like a downward tug that wants our appetites and affections, our passions, to control us. As Paul describes so succinctly in Romans 7:15, "I do not do what I want, but I do the very thing I hate."

As for what we do, Genesis 3:5-6 does a pretty good job of summing that up.

## The Evil That Men Do

In Genesis 3, we hear that "when the woman saw that the tree was good for food, and that it was a delight to the eyes, and that the tree was to be desired to make one wise, she took of its fruit and ate" (Gen 3:6).

If we look closely at that passage, we can see that three things tempted the woman to disobedience: (1) the fruit was "good for food"; (2) it was also a "delight to the eyes"; and (3) it "was to be desired to make one wise."

Those same temptations are later spelled out for us in
1 John 2:15-17, the scriptural passage where the Church
finds the original teaching on concupiscence:

> Do not love the world or the things in the world. If
> any one loves the world, love for the Father is not in
> him. For all that is in the world, the lust of the flesh
> and the lust of the eyes and the pride of life, is not of
> the Father but is of the world. And the world passes
> away, and the lust of it; but he who does the will of
> God abides forever.

The lust of the flesh, the lust of the eyes, and the pride of
life; pleasure, possessions, pride; food, alcohol, drugs, fornica-
tion, adultery, pornography; money, clothes, cars, jewelry, gad-
getry; fame, applause, ignorance, our way, our will, our anger,
and the thirst for revenge — those are the temptations that
pull us away from God. There is no pursuing them both; in
the end, you either love God as a Father or you love the world,
seeing it, not heaven, as your true home.

Recognizing that as the choice before us — between loving God or loving the world — should change the way we
think of sin. It should help us grasp that sin is so much more
than broken laws. It's broken lives. It's broken hearts. It's broken homes. And it is all that because the laws of God are not
arbitrarily imposed.

God, as our Creator, knows us better than we know ourselves. And God, as our Father, loves us better than we love
ourselves. He only legislates what he knows will perfect us
and fulfill us. His laws are for our good, not his. That is to say,
when we sin, we don't really break his laws; we break ourselves against his laws.

We all understand how God's laws work in the physical

order. We know that if Congress got together tomorrow and unanimously passed a law repealing gravity, then decided to go to the White House and jump off the roof, our fine senators and representatives would not fly. They would not break the law of gravity. Rather, the law of gravity would break their bones.

Well, just as the laws of God are firmly fixed in the physical order, they are equally fixed in the spiritual order. Moral laws are no more subject to negotiation than physical laws. When we steal, lie, commit adultery, or fornicate, we don't only disobey our Father. We disobey our perfect, loving Father, doing the very things he told us would hurt us. The negative effects that follow aren't how God punishes us. They're us experiencing the consequences of our failure to trust God. They're us experiencing what happens when we choose not to do what is good for us.

## DIVINE SONSHIP

The fourth chapter of Matthew's Gospel brings home the depths of that choice.

When Christ goes out into the wilderness and fasts for forty days, he faces those same three temptations we face in life — the lust of the flesh, the lust of the eyes, and the pride of life.

First, the devil urges him to turn stones into bread (Mt 4:3). That is pleasure, the lust of the flesh. Then, Satan tells Jesus to prove his divinity: "If you are the Son of God, throw yourself down; for it is written, 'He will give his angels charge of you' " (Mt 4:6). That is the pride of life, putting God to the test and desiring to show your own greatness. Finally, he promises Christ "the kingdoms of the world" (Mt 4:8-9). That is possessiveness, the lust of the eyes.

Were all these temptations? Yes. Christ didn't have concupiscence, but he had a mortal body and a passable nature. He was capable of suffering, dying, and, in the interim, hungering, starving, and thirsting. He faced all the essential temptations that Adam faced in the Garden and that we face now in the world.

But Jesus didn't succumb to those temptations. Through his own self-mastery, as well as his detachment and humility, he held fast to God. He passed the test that Adam failed. And the reason he passed is because he responded as a son. He acted with the trust of a son. As the *Catechism* says in paragraph 538: "At the end of this time Satan tempts him three times, seeking to compromise his filial attitude toward God."

Satan failed. He may have snuffed out the life of divine sonship in Adam, but he missed his target with Christ, the new Adam, the trusting Son.

~

Satan's failed attempt in the wilderness illuminates for us that the essential mystery of our iniquity is not just distrusting God; it is distrusting God as a Father who calls us to something even greater than an Edenic paradise. It is the refusal of divine sonship. It is the refusal of that for which we were made — a life and love so much greater than anything we can find in this world.

And for that refusal, a price had to be paid.

# Chapter 11

~

# RESTORED TO LIFE:
# THE WORK OF ATONEMENT

I'VE NEVER MUCH BEEN A READER OF MYSTERY NOVELS. At night, when the house is quiet, you'll more likely find me sitting down with a book by Joseph Ratzinger than a thriller by Agatha Christie.

One of my neighbors, however, is an avid mystery fan. She can't get enough of them. At least part of the reason for that, she once explained to me, is because there's always an answer at the end — a clear, simple solution to the puzzle the book presents.

That is the difference between divine mysteries and human mysteries. Human mysteries are problems to be solved. They're finite. They're explainable. They can be answered in two hundred pages or less.

Divine mysteries, however, are infinite. They're truths we can come to understand more deeply, but never fully grasp, not in one lifetime or ten, let alone two hundred pages.

The New Testament itself tells us as much.

## Metaphors and Mysteries

When we read through the New Testament, we encounter the human authors conveying supernatural truths in natural terms. In this, they imitate God. God created a world full of natural things — mountains, seas, and hummingbirds — that in some way reveal supernatural truths. They don't reveal all there is to know about those truths, but they nevertheless give us an entry point to grasping them more fully.

What's true in creation is true in salvation history. God explains the supernatural through the natural. He uses the known — human families, human love, and human emotions — to help us understand the unknown.

Accordingly, when the authors of the New Testament talk about Christ's death and what it accomplished, they draw from an arsenal of words and concepts that seem disparate — justification, sanctification, propitiation, expiation, redemption, atonement, sacrifice — but that are all connected to the ancient Israelites' understanding of family.

The thread that connects them is the notion of covenant.

A covenant is a sacred, lasting bond of kinship. Covenants make families. They forge ties deeper and more enduring than blood or biology. In ancient Israel, this notion of covenant shaped family life. The marriage covenant, the bond between husband and wife, was the core of family life — but family went beyond one couple, beyond even children, aunts, uncles, cousins, and grandparents.

For Israel, the family was a clan, the clan was part of a tribe, and the tribe was part of a nation. And because the nation was as much one's family as one's own brothers and sisters, bound up with the understanding of covenant was a vision of a family as an economic unit, a military unit, and a juridical unit. It's that vision that worked its way into the language biblical authors used to talk about Christ's saving death.

Because we no longer think of family in those terms, that connection can be difficult to see when we read Scripture. It also doesn't help that when it comes to the atonement, no one word the biblical authors use, or even all the words together, can convey the fullness of the mystery. The analogies can only go so far. The depths simply can't be plumbed.

That's not to say that divine mysteries such as the Trinity or Christ's death are unreasonable. The mysteries of the faith are always reasonable. They don't go against reason. Rather, they go beyond reason. Faith illuminates reason, helping us grasp truths we could never grasp by reason alone. But unlike human mysteries, the more we ponder these divine mysteries, the greater — not the lesser — the mysteries seem. They are truths truly inexhaustible.

It's important to see that difference because few things in life are more important than understanding what happened on Calvary. But if we don't recognize the underlying notion of covenant and the limits of human language, we can fall into some of the same theological traps our Protestant brothers and sisters have fallen into over the years, traps that obscure rather than illuminate the mystery of Christ's death and resurrection, as well as the love of the Father and the life for which he created us.

## A God Who Atones

As a Protestant, I was introduced to any number of different models used to explain Christ's death on the cross. All are metaphors that draw on the covenant language used by the biblical authors to explain the event. Most of these models will sound somewhat familiar to Catholics, mainly because in our own society Protestants have been more assertive than Catholics about evangelization. So, how they approach the atonement has, to an extent, infiltrated our own thinking about it.

Of those models or metaphors, four dominate.

First is the *Marketplace Model*. Sometimes referred to as the Economic Model, the Marketplace Model focuses on how Christ's death redeems us — or buys us back — from sin. "You were bought with a price," St. Paul tells us in 1 Corinthians 7:23. The word he uses there was also commonly used to talk about buying a slave or securing the freedom of a captive. It implies an economic transaction and reminds us that through our sin we incurred a debt to God, a debt we could not pay. So Christ paid it for us.

Next comes the *Courtroom Model*, or the *Juridical Model*. According to this model, the human race is like a defendant found guilty of a crime in court. The punishment for that crime is death. But the defendant doesn't have to endure the punishment. Rather, it's borne instead by an innocent man who walked into the courtroom and offered himself to the judge. That, say proponents of the courtroom model, is what Christ did for us. He took on our punishment as his own. "They are justified by his grace as a gift ..." (Rom 3:24).

Note, however, according to this model, Christ doesn't take on our guilt. We're still guilty. We're still criminals. We just don't have to pay the price. We're justified by Christ's sacrifice, but no less rotten for it.

Then, there's the *Battlefield Model*. An important metaphor in the early Church, the Battlefield Model recognizes that, on the cross, Christ defeated the devil. He thwarted Satan's plan, winning the spiritual equivalent of a military victory and liberating us — prisoners of war or a conquered people — from bondage, captivity, and the devil's dominion. "The Lord will rescue me from every evil and save me for his heavenly kingdom," writes Paul in 2 Timothy 4:18. Elsewhere he urges Christians to suit up for ongoing spiritual warfare with the command to "put on the whole armor of God" (cf. Eph 6:10-17).

Lastly, we find the *Temple Model*, a model identified by Protestants but one which they never seem quite sure what to do with. This model is rooted in the notion of sacrifice and priesthood and takes its cue from the language of sanctification and expiation. Just as in the Old Testament, Israel atoned for its sins through animal sacrifices offered by Levitical priests in the Temple, so in the New Testament, Christ offers himself as both priest and sacrifice on Calvary. That offering purifies the Church's members, who "have washed their robes and made them white in the blood of the Lamb" (Rev 7:14).

## A GOD OF JUSTICE

From two of those models — the Courtroom Model and the Marketplace Model — the idea of penal substitution has emerged as Protestants' (and some Catholics') primary tool for explaining Jesus' atoning death. According to that idea, humanity deserves nothing less than God's wrath for our sin. But Christ, by stepping in and bearing that wrath for us, appeases that wrath. That is called propitiation.

At first, the idea sounds good. But when you look at it a little more closely, problems emerge.

Problem Number One: Penal Substitution tells us that when God the Father looked at Christ on the cross, he didn't see his Son. He didn't see Christ. He only saw our sin. But how is that possible? How could the all loving Father, who has known and loved his Son through all eternity, not love him on the cross? How could he not see him? How schizophrenic would the First Person of the Trinity have to be to suddenly not know his own Son?

Problem Number Two: Penal substitution heaps all the punishment for our sin upon one victim. Not because he is guilty. Not because he shares any part of our sin. He doesn't. He is the only person truly and totally innocent. Rather, he bears the punishment because he chooses to bear it. In reality, this only compounds humanity's guilt. It's not enough that we had to make such a mess of things. We also had to go and allow an innocent person to pay the price for our mess. Executing a blameless man so that the guilty can go free is a grave injustice that only compounds our guilt. And it doesn't make it any better that the judge allowing it is God. It makes him part of the injustice.

Problem Number Three: Penal substitution tells us that Christ served as our substitute. He bore the punishment for our sin. But if that's the case, why do we still bear the consequences for our sin? Why do we still suffer and die? Shouldn't Christ's suffering have eliminated the need for all that?

What emerges from the idea of penal substitution is a caricature of a blind and wrathful God who visits vengeance upon his innocent Son. What kind of God is that? How do we love him? How do we trust him?

The answer is, we can't. We can't see that God as children see their father. We can only see him as slaves see their master — a hard, cruel, unjust master. But that's not who God is. That's not what God is — and to assert that picture of him borders on blasphemy.

Yet, the fact remains: Jesus paid a debt he did not owe because we owed a debt we could not pay. So how do we reconcile God's acceptance of that payment with a good and loving God? How can what happened on Calvary testify to both God's justice and God's mercy?

## A GOD NOT LIKE US

We start by letting go of the idea that "the wrath of God" of which the Bible speaks (168 times to be exact) is like our wrath. It's not. God is immutable. He's eternal and unchanging. Which means God doesn't get angry. He doesn't experience changing passions or fleeting emotions.

Then why do we find references to God's wrath throughout the Old Testament? For the same reasons we find references to God's "right hand" or "holy arm." God doesn't have limbs any more than he has human emotions, but the human authors of Scripture use those terms as metaphors to convey some truth about God. They apply human characteristics to help us grasp divine truths. As St. Thomas Aquinas explains, "When Scripture speaks of God's arm, the literal sense is not that God has such a member but only what is signified by that member — namely, operative power."[46]

In a similar way, Aquinas argues, when the Bible speaks of God's wrath, it suggests a relationship where one party has wronged another, and the one who has erred experiences the weight of his or her actions through the anger of the other. In other words, God's wrath is a figurative or anthropomorphic expression that describes how an impenitent sinner, who refuses God's mercy, experiences his holy and just love.

God's wrath, in other words, is a figure of speech that points to something real: how we experience God's holy love and his loving justice. Whenever a sinner refuses divine mercy, the fire of God's love burns and is experienced as wrath. Sinners feel the fire of his love and justice, but because they reject both, the fire burns rather than warms. God doesn't stop loving that person or love that person less, but the love they reject feels alien to their soul.

God does not have pent-up wrath that he let loose on Calvary. He has no need to exact vengeance. He doesn't unleash the fires of heaven and hell on his beloved Son in some vindictive fit of passion, all so he can feel better.

If not that, though, then what?

## A GOD OF THE COVENANT

Pope Benedict XVI gave us an answer to that question in an essay entitled "Vicarious Representation." As he makes clear, what Christ did on the cross was not substitutionary. Rather, it was "representative" and "participatory."[47]

On Calvary, Benedict writes, Jesus died as our covenant representative. He is to his people what fathers are to families: their representative. That's why when fathers die, leaving large debts behind, creditors track down their families and demand payment from them. Or, if a father dies leaving money behind, his descendants receive that money as an inheritance. That happens because the actions of the representative devolve upon those covenantally united to him. In a similar way, God has "re-presented" himself in us: His life, his love, and his nature and being were all made present in us from the moment he begat us. That's what paternity is.

From Jesus' perspective, what he did was representative. From our perspective, however, it was participatory. We recognize that we are particular members of one family. We are parts of a whole, of a body, and as parts of a body we participate in the actions of its head, of Christ. Christ's obedience as a Son, his love, his suffering, and his death are reproduced or re-presented in us.

The Incarnation made this participation possible. Writing in the fourth century, St. Gregory of Nazianzus explained that Christ assumed our whole nature, not just part of it, because "whatever is not assumed is not redeemed."[48] Christ assumed our whole human nature so that he could impart his whole nature to us. "The Son of God becomes the Son of Man so that sons of men may become the sons of God."[49] That's not deifying humans. It's filiation. It is imparting to us a share in Christ's own divine sonship, making us children of God.

What God the Father wanted when Jesus hung on the cross, what he has always wanted from the first moment he spoke to man in the Garden, was filial love. In the Garden, he wanted man to obey him not out of fear or necessity but out of a loving trust in God's perfect goodness and will. Adam, our first covenant representative, refused to give that in the Garden. But Christ, our new covenant representative, gave that on the cross. Having taken on our human nature in the Incarnation, he offered his life in loving obedience to the Father.

## A GOD OF MERCY AND LOVE

What happened on Calvary wasn't a revelation of God's vengeance. It was a revelation of the inner life of the Trinity. On Good Friday, Christ did what he has always done: the Father looked down on him with Love (which is the life of the Godhead, the Holy Spirit), Jesus received that Love, and then imaged the Father by pouring Love back in return to him.

Then, when at last Jesus gave up his *pneuma* — his breath — water and blood flowed from his pierced side as visible signs of the invisible mysteries of Baptism and the Eucharist, mysteries which communicate life to us. Through the sacraments, we receive God's life. We receive what Jesus imparted to us through his incarnation, passion, death, and resurrection. We participate in his atoning act of Sonship, and we receive the grace to bear our crosses, completing "what is lacking in Christ's afflictions for the sake of his body, that is, the Church" (Col 1:24).

The representative and participatory nature of Christ's death empowers us to carry those crosses, endowing our sufferings with a redemptive value they would never have on their own. The moment we imitate Christ on the cross — a Christ who never looked more beautiful to the Father than when he offered himself with such loving trust — and accept the crosses that come our way with the same trust, our crosses become sanctifying. They become redemptive.

So, through the cross God reveals not wrath, not vindictive hatred, not a desire to punish, but rather a mercy that does not compromise justice and a justice that is ordered to mercy. On the cross, the love of Christ overcomes the hard, cold sin within our hearts, as the hot sun overcomes hard ice. If sin is a rejection of divine sonship, Christ's atoning sacrifice is the supreme reassertion of divine sonship, a reassertion of filial love that takes sin out at its source — our shortsighted, foolish, prideful refusal to love and trust as a child.

~

This is what we need to understand in order to grow in love with God. It's also what we need to communicate to those who want to follow God but soon discover that the more we strive to follow Christ, the more of our own weaknesses and failures we see. That growing sense of sin can be overwhelming if not matched with an understanding that God's "anger" is not the opposite of his love but an expression of his love. It's how we experience his love when we turn our backs on it.

That understanding becomes even clearer when we understand the fullness of the familial relationship to which God calls us.

# Chapter 12

~

# His by Covenant:
# The Family of God

God loves us. As Catholics, we say we know that. And when we proclaim the Gospel, that's the first truth we proclaim. But in order to grasp the depths of that love, we have to understand that salvation is about more than being forgiven.

About fifteen years ago, I said that to a Protestant pastor in the middle of a radio interview, and he looked at me as if I had said the earth was flat.

"What do you mean salvation is about more than being forgiven?" he asked.

Searching for an analogy that would make my point, I told him about a recent encounter I had with Bill, my mechanic.

"Last week I had car trouble and took it to the service station near where I live," I explained. "Bill identified two problems, so I left it there, came back the next day, paid for the repairs, and took the car home. But on the drive, I realized he had only completed one repair. I drove it back and handed over the keys to Bill. He apologized, of course, and I said, 'I forgive you.' But I didn't drive him home. I didn't write him into my will and make him a part of our family. I just forgave him.'"

After I finished, Don, the pastor interviewing me, still had the same quizzical look on his face, so I gave it another try.

## A Pardon Like No Other

"Picture a man who has committed a series of heinous crimes," I told him. "He's been sentenced to death for those crimes and has run out of appeals. To make matters worse, he has a terminal illness. So, even if he weren't facing the chair, his days are numbered. The day for his execution comes. But moments before the executioner carries out the sentence, the governor calls. He's pardoning the criminal.

"On the one hand, the criminal feels relieved. On the other hand, he's still a dying man. Besides, all his legal appeals have bankrupted him, and he is totally alone in the world — no friends, no family, no one. To him, his life doesn't seem worth saving.

"Before he even has time to process that, however, the governor says, 'Wait. There's more. Not only am I granting you a pardon, but scientists have discovered a cure for your disease, and there's a doctor waiting outside the prison doors to administer it. I've also paid off all your debts, and when you get out of prison, you'll see a big white limousine waiting for you. It will bring you to my home, where you will live as my son. I've already filled out the adoption papers and written you into my will, so you will inherit all I have right along with my other children.

"That's what God has done for us," I concluded. "That's what I mean when I say salvation is about so much more than forgiveness."

Don was still staring at me. By now, however, his look was one of astonishment.

"Why have I never heard this before?" he asked.

To that question, I didn't have an answer. I did know, however, that he wasn't alone. Many Protestants (and Catholics too) only think about Christ's death on the cross in terms of what it spared us. They see God's love made manifest in his forgiveness. And God's love *is* made manifest in his forgiveness. But the fullness of his mercy and love, the extent of his greatness and glory, and the extravagance of his grace don't shine forth in the pardon he extends to us. It shines forth in the relationship and the life to which he calls us. It shines forth in his invitation to divine sonship, to become partakers in his own life.

## A Model Family

In the mid-1940s, the great Harvard sociologist Carle Zimmerman set a team of young scholars to work analyzing family structure in nearly every known civilization and age. He published that research in his book *Family and Civilization*, where he concluded that in all of human history, three different types of families have existed: the trustee family, the domestic family, and the atomistic family.[50]

"The trustee family," Zimmerman writes, "is so named because it more or less considers itself as immortal, existing in perpetuity, and never being extinguished."

He goes on to explain that the living members of the trustee family see themselves as trustees, almost like the trustees of a corporation. As they understand it, their family existed before they were born and will continue existing after their death. They are simply the custodians of its "blood, rights, property, name, and position" during their lifetime.[51]

According to Zimmerman, trustee families are also essentially religious in nature, with all family members — past, present, and future — believing they form one mystical organism united by a sacred trust. Within the trustee family, members see marriage as a sacred covenant, and recognize children as a blessing from the gods. They also believe fathers have both priestly and kingly authority and call them to lead their families in worship, as well as help govern.

Given all that, it makes sense that trustee families view sexual immorality, especially adultery, which breaks the sacred covenant of marriage, as a crime, punishable by death.

When it comes to domestic families, Zimmerman tells us that their members understand themselves as participating in an important moral tradition, not a mystical organism. Domestic families are based on the marital bond and consist of the husband, the wife, and their children, but the bond that unites husband and wife is seen more as a contract than a covenant. It is a legal bond, not a sacred one. Similarly, domestic families see children not so much as blessings but as economic agents who will inherit and work the family property, while fathers are like CEOs, heads of an economic unit. This understanding of family emphasizes the duty of family members to one another and, albeit to a lesser extent, individual rights. Accordingly, sexual immorality is still considered a sin, but not a crime.

Once you get to the atomistic family, however, individual rights have primacy. What the individual wants or thinks himself entitled to is exalted above family duties or responsibility, and the family itself exists for the sake of the individual's pleasure. In some ways, societies where the atomistic family dominates see the family almost as a cocoon, from which the individual must work to emerge — true freedom existing only outside the family.

Atomistic families downgrade marriage as well. No longer understood either as a sacred covenant or a binding contract, marriage becomes a voluntary association of convenience for the purpose of companionship. It's a relationship that can be entered or abandoned at will. No questions asked. Children also matter less in the atomistic family, becoming liabilities, rather than assets or blessings. The state usurps the father's role, and sexual immorality loses any stigma. It becomes just one more choice for the individual to make.

## RISE AND FALL

Those three different classifications of families weren't all that Zimmerman's research turned up. He also observed that in the whole of world history the only societies that ever became identifiable as "civilizations" all started out as trustee families. Only trustee-family societies ever became big enough and strong enough and lasted long enough to rise to the level of a civilization.

Rome is the perfect example of this. When you look at pre-imperial Rome — in the fifth or sixth century B.C. — what you see is a tribal extended family, with fathers who have both priestly and kingly authority.

With Rome, however, as with every other trustee-family society that emerged as a civilization, the foundation didn't last. Eventually, it devolved into a domestic family society. When that happened, the family co-existed alongside an ever-growing state, a state that gradually assumed the responsibilities once held by the trustee family: healthcare, education, the care of the poor, and so forth.

Without a religious vision to hold the domestic family together, however, it, too, never lasts. Zimmerman's research found that domestic-family societies rarely last more than a century or two, as they quickly devolve into atomistic family societies. This is the third and final stage for once great civilizations, the stage that heralds the civilization's impending collapse. In those civilizations, wherever they might be — Africa, Asia, India, or Europe — the same phenomena occur as the atomistic family takes hold of society: widespread divorce, unrestrained sexual activity, and population decline.

Why is all this important?

On one level, Zimmerman's research helps us understand the state of our society today, as the once primary model of the domestic family gives way to the atomistic model. He shows us where we are in the trajectory all great civilizations follow. Unfortunately, the news is not good.

Even more fundamentally, Zimmerman's thesis helps clear away the modern conceptions of family that can cloud our understanding of who God is and to what he calls us. It reminds us that the way most people view marriage today — as an oftentimes temporary association of adults forged in desire and broken when desire dissipates — is not how our ancestors viewed marriage. It also reminds us that family life doesn't have to be a burden or an occasion for woundedness. It can be a source of divine blessing, ordered to loving sacrifice and holy communion.

And in that, Zimmerman's thesis gives the post-modern mind an entry point for understanding Jesus' call in the Scriptures to the family of God.


## A TRINITY


As we've already discussed, during his earthly ministry, Jesus shocked his Jewish contemporaries by freely referring to God as "Father" or "*Abba*" ("Daddy"). But that's not the only way his language stunned his listeners. As Jesus went about Israel, proclaiming the Kingdom, he also made the most shocking of claims: "I and the Father are one" (Jn 10:30); "He who has seen me has seen the Father" (Jn 14:9); "I am in the Father and the Father is in me" (Jn 14:11).

All these claims, in some way, implied that Jesus was equal to God. He was equally wise, equally powerful, and equally good. If Jesus was all that, possessing in equal measure all the divine attributes of God the Father in heaven, that meant Jesus *was* God.

As his public ministry continued, the news became even more unsettling. In God, there wasn't just the Father and the Son. There was also a Third Person: the Holy Spirit. At the Last Supper, Jesus spoke of "the Counselor, the Holy Spirit, whom the Father will send in my name, he will teach you all things, and bring to your remembrance all that I have said to you" (Jn 14:26). He also charged his disciples to baptize "in the name of the Father and of the Son and of the Holy Spirit" (Mt 28:19).

The truth that Jesus revealed is the truth John Paul II spoke of on his first papal visit to the Americas. He said, "God in his deepest mystery is not a solitude but a family because God has in himself fatherhood, sonship, and the essence of the family — which is love."[52] That love, of course, isn't a thing. It's a Person: the Holy Spirit.

Note: John Paul II doesn't say that God is *like* a family. He says that God *is* a family. God possesses from all eternity the fundamental attributes of a family — fatherhood, sonship, and love — and he possesses them in their perfection. In some ways, it would be more accurate to say our families, yours and mine, are "like" a family. As I know all too well, the Hahns have fatherhood, but as my kids will tell you, it's a flawed fatherhood. We also have sonship, but as I can prove, it's flawed for them too. We don't possess the attributes of family in their perfection. Only God does that. He *is* family. The rest of us are just imperfect imitators.

## A CHURCH

Jesus, through his preaching and ministry, revealed to us that God is a Family. Then he went a step further. In calling people to follow him, Jesus called them to a family that surpassed even the tribal family in importance.

That's what Israel was. It was a society that perfectly mirrored what Zimmerman described as a tribal family. But Jesus said it wasn't enough: there was a family whose importance and claims surpassed that of Israel's: "Whoever does the will of God is my brother, and sister, and mother" (Mk 3:31-35). Even more shockingly: "If any one comes to me and does not hate his own father and mother and wife and children and brothers and sisters, yes, and even his own life, he cannot be my disciple" (Lk 14:26).

In that, Jesus revealed to Israel God's ultimate plan for them and for the whole human race.

Going back to Zimmerman for a minute, it helps to remember that his research concluded that no civilization which began as a tribal family ever managed to stay that way. The tribal-family system always devolved into a domestic-family system, then an atomistic-family system, and finally the civilization collapsed.

When I discovered Zimmerman's research in the 1980s, it disturbed me. I couldn't understand why God, being God and having the power to unite people, wouldn't do so. Why would he allow tribal family after tribal family to collapse? You'd think at least one privileged civilization would emerge from the whole mess.

Eventually, I came to understand that one did.

The Bible is the history of that family. It's a family that began with a marriage in the Garden, with Adam and Eve. It grew into a household with Noah, a tribe with Abraham, a nation with Moses, and an international kingdom with David.

Finally, in Christ, the family became what it was always meant to be: the universal family of God, the Catholic Church.

By establishing the New Covenant, Christ founded the one universal family of God. The tribal family is like that family in the same way that the Hahn family is like the family of God. It possesses the fundamental elements but not in their perfection. It gives an entry point to understanding the Church, but it is surpassed by the real thing.

## A FAMILY

The Church is God's family because it is Christ's Body, an extension of the incarnate Christ, and, as such, an extension of the Trinity's own life. It is one, because a man's greatness consists in his capacity to father one family. We call a man who fathers more than one family a scoundrel, an adulterer. But God is not a scoundrel. His glory is in fathering one universal family and maintaining its oneness.

That's why Catholics can say with confidence that the Church is the universal family of God "outside [of which] there is no salvation" (see CCC, nn. 846-848). That teaching doesn't condemn anybody. It simply clarifies how we understand the meaning of salvation — that it is more than getting out of hell; it is more than not being condemned. It is an invitation to participate in God's own family life.

The more time passes, the more convinced I've become that the family of God is the master idea behind the Catholic faith.

When you come to Catholicism, you find a beautiful mansion with many rooms, many doors, and many locks. Not only to get in, but to get through the whole house and understand its interior unity and inner-connectedness — the mystery of the Trinity, the spiritual motherhood of Mary, the role of the saints, the power of the sacraments — you must see the Church as a family.

Many men and women have a conversion experience to a personal relationship with Jesus, but once the initial experience passes, they're just running on the fumes of warm and fuzzy feelings. Those feelings might last for a few hours or days or even years. But eventually they wear off, leaving the person wondering if the experience was real. In a sense, people who find themselves in that state are like children wondering who they really are or if they truly know their parents.

In our human families, we have objective experiences that answer that question for us. Birthdays and anniversaries, family meals and family vacations, a street address and a bedroom — all tell us that we belong to a particular family. The same holds true in the family of God.

As Catholics, we have the saints and the sacraments, feast days and penitential seasons, doctrine and liturgy, all of which structure our life and keep us constantly connected to our Father in heaven. Even the names we use — calling priests "Father," nuns "Sister," or their abbess "Mother Superior" — reflect this familial vision of Church. And this spiritual family isn't less familial than our natural family: it's arguably more familial, more real, because it's the Trinitarian sacramental bond that joins us to one another. It's a family forged by the bond that other family bonds only image.

## Salvation in the Here and Now

To be outside of the Church is to be outside of God's family. That is what we need to be saved from. That is also the key to unlocking the statement we hear at the climax of John's Gospel during the Last Supper: "I am the way, and the truth, and the life; no one comes to the Father, but by me" (Jn 14:6).

On one hand, that statement seems strange. Men and women had been coming to God apart from Christ since the dawn of creation. They continue to do so today. But what those people were and are doing is approaching God as Paul saw the Athenians, with their landscape littered with altars, approaching God (Acts 17). They were approaching a God they didn't know, and they weren't approaching him as children but strictly in creaturely terms, as servants would approach their master.

Again, "No one comes to the *Father* but by me." That is the point. God's paternity is nothing other than a figure of speech until the Incarnation. Nobody knows God as Father apart from Christ. And nobody can reach the mystery of his paternity and his divine love apart from Christ.

That means we have to stop thinking of all religions as different paths up the same mountain. As the Hinduologist Paul Hacker stressed: Islam, Hinduism, Taoism — these are not different paths. They're different mountains. It's not all relative.

That doesn't mean non-Catholics or non-Christians won't make it to heaven. But it also doesn't make it so that salvation is nothing more than getting to heaven. Salvation is not just then and there. It's here and now. Salvation is for experiencing the fullness of the life and love of the Father, the Son, and the Holy Spirit. And we don't have to wait until we get to heaven to experience that.

When we are baptized, the Holy Spirit comes to dwell in us. We are adopted. We are reborn. We are made members of the family that God has been fathering since the beginning. Then, through the other sacraments, the family of God is sustained. It's nourished by the life and love of God himself, a life given with new power in Confirmation, with sustaining grace in Marriage, with transforming grace in Holy Orders, and with healing grace in the Anointing of the Sick. Throughout our lives, when we receive the Eucharist, God's life grows in us; family ties are strengthened. And when we break those family ties through sin, we avail ourselves of the Sacrament of Penance.

## THE SACRAMENT OF THE NEW EVANGELIZATION

Ultimately, that's the tragedy of sin — not just original sin but actual sin: the ordinary ways we stumble and fall every day. Sin is broken covenant fellowship. It is broken covenant relations. It is a failure to love as sons and daughters are called to love.

Fortunately for us, there's a remedy for sin: confession. In a sense, the Sacrament of Penance is *the* Sacrament of the New Evangelization. We hear again and again that the best way to grow in holiness is to frequent the sacraments. But there are only two sacraments we can receive frequently. One is the Eucharist. The other is the Sacrament of Penance.

If we want to be more and more conformed to Christ, even daily Communion isn't enough. Every day we also must take a long hard look at ourselves, a look that needs to grow longer and harder with each passing year, and see where we're failing to trust God as our Father, where we're failing to live up to the call to divine sonship. Then, we have to humble ourselves and go to confession, at least every month, if not more.

That's not easy. Who wants to go back to the priest, week after week, year after year, and keep admitting how far short we continue to fall of the grace we've been given? Not me. Not any of us. But God wants us to come. He wants to restore to us the grace we've lost through sin. And he wants us to come as often as it takes to overcome whatever habitual sin prevents us from living the fullness of divine sonship. As Pope

Francis said at his first Angelus, just days after his election: "The Lord never tires of forgiving. It is we who tire of asking for forgiveness."[53]

~

The Catholic Church is in no way incidental to salvation. To belong to her, to be alive in Christ through her, is to participate in God saving us through the Son by the power of the Holy Spirit. It is also to belong to a family that doesn't just stretch across the globe but stretches from earth to heaven. In heaven, she exists in perfection. Here, the imperfections of her members seemingly mar her beauty. But she is still one Church, undivided in body and soul, fathered by God through history and made manifest by Christ with the institution of the New Covenant in the Eucharist.

That brings us to the final truth we need to plumb in order to fully grasp the Gospel we proclaim in the New Testament: how an execution became a sacrifice, and how a meal became a participation in that sacrifice.

# Chapter 13

~

# TRANSFORMED BY LOVE:
# FROM SUPPER TO SACRIFICE

"WHERE IN THE NEW TESTAMENT do you find the Holy Sacrifice of the Mass?"

Back in high school, when I was an enthusiastic new convert to evangelical Christianity, I put that question over and over again to my Catholic classmates. I thought of it as my "gotcha" question, an irrefutable proof that the Church of Rome had it all wrong.

Most of my classmates didn't see it that way: the lunchroom of Upper St. Clair High School wasn't exactly filled with Catholic teens dropping to their knees to pray the Sinner's Prayer. But I kept asking the question just the same. I was convinced that in order to lead people to a relationship with Christ, I had to lead them away from the Eucharist. I believed a love for the two couldn't co-exist.

Looking back now, I know I couldn't have been more wrong.

The fact is, there can be no true evangelization without the Eucharist. It's not simply that the Eucharist is the context in which evangelization unfolds or even the goal of evangelization. It's the content of evangelization. It's what we proclaim when we evangelize, and it's what makes our efforts at evangelization fruitful.

## MORE THAN A MEAL

"Jesus did not redeem the world with beautiful words, but with his suffering and death," then Cardinal Ratzinger said to a group of catechists in 2000. "His Passion is the inexhaustible source of life for the world; the Passion gives power to his words…. Whoever omits the cross, omits the essence of Christianity (see 1 Cor 2:2)."[54]

As a Protestant, I would have agreed with that. But what I didn't understand then is that without the Eucharist you can't understand the cross. If you omit the cross, you omit the essence of Christianity. If you omit the Eucharist, however, you omit what explains how Christ's death became the means to our salvation.

Like other Protestants, when I read the account of the Last Supper, I saw Jesus instituting a meal, not a sacrifice. What took place on Calvary was the sacrifice. From my point of view, they were two separate events with two separate meanings.

The more I read the Church Fathers, however, the more I realized that I was looking at those events with the eyes of a twentieth-century Protestant. If I had stood on Calvary that day as a devout first-century Jew, watching Jesus suffer and die, I wouldn't have gone home and told my friends I had just witnessed a sacrifice. Sacrifices took place within Jerusalem, in the Temple, on an altar, with a priest. But Jesus died outside the walls, far from the Temple, with no altars or priests.

No, what I would have told my friends is that I had just witnessed a Roman execution — and a bloody one at that. From a Jewish perspective, that's what Jesus' death was. So how does a Roman execution become a holy sacrifice? And not just any holy sacrifice but the supreme sacrifice of all time?

To find the answer to that question, we need to rewind the tape and look at what took place in the Upper Room on Holy Thursday. There, Jesus didn't just institute a meal or celebrate the Passover supper one last time. He fulfilled the Passover supper as the Lamb of God, transforming it from the Passover of the Old Testament into the Passover of the New.

In the context of celebrating the ancient Passover ritual, he took bread and spoke the words, "This is my Body, which will be given up for you."

At the time, the disciples had to wonder what he meant by that. They had been celebrating the Passover all their lives. They knew the ritual like the back of their hands — and those words did not belong there. They weren't part of the tradition. Upon first hearing, Jesus' words couldn't have made much sense to them.

The situation became even more confusing at the end of the meal, when Jesus took the third cup of blessing and said, "This is the chalice of my Blood, the Blood of the new and eternal covenant, which will be poured out for you and for many."

Again, the disciples must have scratched their heads, wondering at these new additions to the Passover rubrics. Was this just empty rhetoric, or did they point to some new reality they couldn't yet comprehend?

## More Than an Execution

The answer to that question became plain just hours later, on Good Friday. On the cross, Jesus' body *was* given up, and his blood *was* poured out. On Calvary, as our high priest, he offered himself as a sacrifice, *the* sacrifice of the New Covenant, *the* Lamb of God.

The two events — the Holy Thursday Passover meal and Christ's death on Calvary — are inextricably connected. They are, in a sense, part of the same event. And the Passover is the key to understanding that.

In the Old Testament, the Passover wasn't simply a meal. Just ask the lamb. It started as a sacrifice and culminated in a meal. If that was true of the Old Covenant Passover, it has to be more true, not less true, of the New Covenant Passover. After all, Jesus came not just as the Lamb of God to feed us but also as the Lamb of God to die for us.

If what took place on Holy Thursday was just a meal, then Christ's death on Good Friday was just an execution. If, however, Jesus' institution of the Holy Eucharist was nothing less than the institution of the New Covenant Passover sacrifice, then and only then was what took place on Good Friday a sacrifice. Calvary is a sacrifice if it's the culmination of Christ giving himself away, not primarily as a victim of injustice but rather as a victim of love.

Which, of course, from the very start, the Church knew it was, with St. Paul writing in 1 Corinthians 5:7-8, "For Christ, our Paschal Lamb has been sacrificed," and enjoining the Christian community to "celebrate the festival" by adhering to the liturgy instituted by Christ on Holy Thursday:

> For I received from the Lord what I also delivered to you, that the Lord Jesus on the night when he was betrayed took bread, and when he had given thanks, he broke it, and said, "This is my body which is for you. Do this in remembrance of me." In the same way also the chalice, after supper, saying, "This chalice is the new covenant in my blood. Do this, as often as you drink it, in remembrance of me." (1 Cor 11:23-25)

## More Than a Sacrifice

The mystery of the Eucharist is what transforms Jesus' suffering from a bloody execution into a holy sacrifice. But what transforms that sacrifice into a sacrament?

The Resurrection.

As Paul tells us in Romans, the Resurrection was necessary because it is the means by which we die and rise to new life in Christ. Again, for Catholics salvation means so much more than being redeemed from sin. It's not just what we're saved from but what we're saved for. It's not just to watch Jesus experience this new resurrected life but also to share in it ourselves:

> We were buried therefore with him by baptism into death, so that as Christ was raised from the dead by the glory of the Father, we too might walk in newness of life. So you must consider yourselves dead to sin and alive to God in Christ Jesus. (Rom 6:4, 11)

In other words, the Resurrection was necessary to complete the work of our salvation.

So often in Protestantism it's said that the death of Jesus and our faith in his atoning sacrifice save us. Yet Paul explicitly states in Romans 4:25 that Jesus was "put to death for our trespasses and raised for our justification." That is to say, Jesus' death is not the only aspect of his saving work. His resurrection is just as essential. Our salvation involves two elements: the payment rendered on the cross for the debt for our sin and his resurrection for the sake of our justification.

Christ's resurrection was not simply for his own sake. It was more than a vindication for him; it was a gift to us, a gift that makes it possible for our humanity to be united to his divinity.

The *Catechism* explains:

> The Paschal Mystery has two aspects: by his death, Christ liberates us from sin; by his Resurrection, he opens for us the way to a new life. This new life is above all justification that reinstates us in God's grace.... Justification consists in both victory over the death caused by sin and a new participation in grace (cf. Eph 2:4-5; 1 Pet 1:3). It brings about filial adoption so that men become Christ's brethren.... We are brethren not by nature, but by the gift of grace, because that adoptive filiation gains us a real share in the life of the only Son, which was fully revealed in his Resurrection. (CCC 654)

And where is that gift given to us? In the Eucharist.

## MORE THAN A RESUSCITATION

Scripture tells us that the resurrection of the Lord's body is so much more than a corpse coming back to life. The Resurrection is the glorification of his sacred humanity — a humanity both deified and deifying. It's also what makes his sacred humanity communicable to us. It's what makes the glorified body, dare we say, edible by us.

In the Eucharist, it is the Resurrected Lord that comes to us. The Holy Sacrifice of the Mass is one and the same sacrifice offered at Calvary, but the Jesus we receive in the Eucharist isn't the bleeding, battered Jesus who hung on the cross. It's Jesus the eternal high priest of heaven and the Lamb of God. In the Mass, he's the one offering, and he's the one offered — and he offers himself not as a reward for our righteousness but as remedy for our sins, our weaknesses, and our failures.

Why does he do that? One reason: Love.

Love is the key to unlocking the Paschal Mystery. Love is the truth that underlies it all — from Holy Thursday to Easter Sunday to a Tuesday-morning Mass at your local parish.

One drop of Jesus' precious blood was enough to redeem the whole human race. One act of obedience was all it took. But Jesus gave so much more than that. He gave everything to pay a debt we couldn't pay. That should have incurred for us an even greater debt. We should owe more in the wake of his passion and death. We should bear a greater guilt. But we don't.

We don't because Christ's love was superabundant. His executioners' malice was great, but his love was greater. The greatness of his love outweighed the murderous guilt of those who crucified him.

Reflecting on that truth, Pope Benedict writes, "The Cross reminds us that there is no true love without suffering, there is no gift of life without pain."[55]

In other words, love without suffering is just empty words or transient emotions. Love is proven by suffering; love is perfected by suffering; and love is purified by suffering. At the same time, though, suffering without love is unendurable. It's love that empowers us to bear what we could never otherwise bear. And it's love that transforms suffering into a sacrifice, a gift freely given.

If Christ's love is what transforms his suffering into a sacrifice, then Holy Thursday is when he institutes the sacrament of love, Good Friday is when he endures the suffering of love, and Easter Sunday is when he provides us with the sacrament that enables us to love in a way that is truly Godlike and to share in a life that is truly divine.

Because of the Resurrection, we can become "partakers of the divine nature" (2 Pet 1:4), at every Mass, every day of our lives.

## MORE THAN A BOOK

This brings us back to the challenge I once issued to my Catholic friends: Where in the books of the New Testament do you find the Sacrifice of the Mass?

Well, according to those very books, I had the whole thing backward. The Holy Sacrifice of the Mass isn't simply *in* the New Testament. It *is* the New Testament. The Eucharist is the New Testament. That's what Jesus himself says in the Gospels as he institutes the Eucharist: "This ... is the new covenant in my blood" (Lk 22:20). The Latin word for covenant used in that verse is *testamentum* — "testament." And the only time those words appear together in the books we call the New Testament is right there.

Not surprisingly, the disciples and the early Fathers followed Christ's example, referring to the Eucharist as the "New Testament." While we don't find a single instance of the books of the New Testament being called "the books of the New Testament" until the second half of the second century, we do hear the Eucharist referred to over and over again as the New Testament starting in the first half of the first century. It was their liturgical proximity to what Christ called the New Testament — the fact that they were read in the Mass where the Eucharist was celebrated — that eventually earned those books their collective title.

Again, however, the Mass came first. This makes sense. After all, at the Last Supper, Jesus didn't say, "Write this in memory of me." He said, "Do this in memory of me." And that's what the disciples did. Only a handful of them authored books of the Bible. But from the beginning, they all celebrated the Mass. They all made Jesus known in the Breaking of the Bread.

~

The New Evangelization will need to take on more than a million different forms because more than a million different people have been de-Christianized. There is no one-size-fits-all formula … except for the Eucharist.

The Eucharist is for all. It illuminates Jesus' suffering on the cross, revealing to us, as St. Thomas Aquinas said, that it isn't how much Jesus suffered on the cross that saves us; it's how much he loved us from the cross. It's the love of the Son, expressed through the obedience of his suffering, that redeems us.

The Eucharist is also what gives us the capacity to love with a love that is not merely natural but supernatural, to enter into the inner logic of God's love and accept suffering, to carry our crosses. Again, the Eucharist is what transforms us into living sacrifices, enabling us to enter into a life that is divine and do what we could never do on our own.

That's why God the Father isn't content to leave his children in some far-off country, simply making a decision to believe in him. He wants everyone to come all the way home, to enter into a covenantal union with him and receive his life through the Eucharist, through the sacrifice of the New Covenant, so that he can evangelize us week after week, making it possible for us to offer our own lives back to him as living sacrifices.

This is what we must proclaim in the New Evangelization. And at every Mass, we're called to discover it for ourselves, to remember it, and to live it anew.

# Chapter 14

~

# LOVE AND FIDELITY: WHAT MATTERS MOST

A FEW FINAL THOUGHTS.

First, as we go forward to do the work of the New Evangelization, we need to guard against an "us vs. them" mentality. In this culture, it's easy to see ourselves as the faithful few braving the condemnation of the secular world in order to proclaim the Gospel to all those fallen souls.

That's not how it works though. It's not "us" trying to reach "them." We are "them." We may not be sinning as boldly as others. But we still sin. We may believe in Christ. But we need to believe in him more.

In this world, we all are fallen. We all are in need of Christ's mercy and grace. We always can love more, trust more, and hope more. Doing the work of the New Evangelization requires that we recognize that. It requires we let ourselves be evangelized, even as we seek to evangelize others. Baptized or not, daily communicant or not, we're still sheep. There's only one shepherd. We are not him.

Second, we need to remember that God calls us to be faithful, not successful. Like that sower of seeds in Matthew 13, our job is to sow seeds with abandon — on rocky ground, along the path, among the thorns, as well as in fertile soil. Then, we need to let God take it from there. We can't stand guard over every seed, waiting to see if it takes root. Nor can we only sow where we know our seeds will most likely bear fruit.

That's tempting. It's tempting to pursue success, to maximize the fruit of our efforts like corporations maximizing their profits. But getting caught up in numbers — numbers of conversions made, numbers of dollars raised, numbers of programs launched — makes us susceptible to two deadly errors.

First, that mind-set leads to seeing our success as just that — "our" success.

In his First Letter to the Corinthians, St. Paul has a few things to say to those who think their smarts or know-how can save the world:

> For the word of the cross is folly to those who are perishing, but to us who are being saved it is the power of God. For it is written, "I will destroy the wisdom of the wise, and the cleverness of the clever I will thwart." Where is the wise man? Where is the scribe? Where is the debater of this age? Has not God made foolish the wisdom of the world? For since, in the wisdom of God, the world did not know God through wisdom, it pleased God through the folly of what we preach to save those who believe. (1 Cor 1:18-21)

What we proclaim — the folly of the cross — is foolishness to those who seek wisdom and a stumbling stone to those looking for signs of power. Who could blame us if we decided to take a pass on that part of the Gospel, right? Wouldn't it make more sense if we just focused on Jesus' public miracles? All the healings, the profound parables, how sinners loved Jesus because he was so nonjudgmental?

The answer is, "Yes. It would make sense … according to the world." But that's not what God calls us to do. He calls us to proclaim the cross, Christ's death and resurrection. He also calls us to take up our own crosses and carry them. To many, that seems like the essence of foolishness. And yet, it's what helps us remember that it's not us saving the world — it's God. He doesn't want us to fall into the sin of pride for one second. That's what happened with Lucifer. And look how well that turned out.

## Imitators of Christ

The second problem with pursuing success or trying to quantify the fruits of the New Evangelization is that it sets us up for disappointment. After all, from an earthly standpoint, Jesus' public ministry didn't turn out to be all that successful.

Back when he was still Cardinal Ratzinger, Benedict XVI wrote of Jesus:

> He died almost abandoned; he was condemned on account of his preaching. The response to his message was not the great Yes of his people, but the Cross. From such an end as that, we should conclude that Success is definitely not one of the names of God and that it is not Christian to have an eye to outward success or numbers. God's paths are other than that: his success comes about through the Cross and is always found under that sign.[56]

I love that: Success is not one of the names of God. If we measured the value of what Jesus did on earth by the number of people who came to believe in him during his lifetime, we would all be in trouble.

Again, fidelity is what God wants from us. He wants us to live the Gospel, and he wants us to proclaim it. He wants us to love him, and he wants us to lead others to his love.

How each of us does that will be different from how everybody else does that. In his introduction to *Rome Sweet Home*, Peter Kreeft says that conversions are like snowflakes: no two are alike.[57] The same can be said about the forms the work of the New Evangelization will take in each of our lives. The work will look different in every home and every parish. How we go about that work is a question for prayer and discernment.

But we do need to go about it.

"Enter by the narrow gate," Jesus tells us. "For the gate is wide and the way is easy, that leads to destruction, and those who enter by it are many. For the gate is narrow and the way is hard, that leads to life, and those who find it are few" (Mt 7:13-14).

That's Jesus' take on the road to heaven: the gate is narrow and those who find it are few.

Our culture's take (a take shared by many Catholics, faithful or otherwise) is just the opposite: the gate to heaven is wide, and those who find it are many.

Nobody knows how many souls are in heaven and how many souls are in hell. That's like asking how many angels can dance on the head of a pin. But if I'm playing the odds, I'm going with Jesus on this one. Heaven is not guaranteed. It's not a sure thing — not for anyone, and especially not for those following the wide, sloping path paved by our culture.

Chances are, people we love are walking down that path. Depending on the day, you or I might be walking down that path ourselves. The New Evangelization tells us that when that happens we have a responsibility to turn ourselves around. We also have a responsibility to try, as best we can, to turn others around. It's not all up to us. Not by a long shot. But God asks us to try just the same, trusting him to do the rest.

Even then, there are no guarantees. As Pope Benedict reminds us, "God accepts man's freedom. He is no magician, who will in the end wipe out everything that has happened and wheel out his happy ending."[58]

No, God is not a magician. He is our Father, our true Father, who doesn't force us to obey or believe or love. He asks us to do it. He promises all the help we need to do it. But, if we choose to say no, he will accept that — even if that no is to him.

In the end, for each of us, it comes down to two things. First, the mortality rate for every man, woman, and child on this earth is 100 percent. It's not a question of if we die, but when we die. Second, at the same time, the immortality rate for every man, woman, and child is also 100 percent. Everyone who has ever lived and died still lives. The Assyrians, the Babylonians, the Romans — they all live on in heaven, hell, or purgatory. They're conscious. They know who they are, they know what they've done, and they know what eternity they face.

One day, we will join them, and we will know the same. We are all going to live forever. The only question is where, and the answer to that question depends on what we do with the days we've been given — how we live, how we love, how we embrace the crosses that come our way.

As Catholics, that is what we believe. We celebrate it at every Mass, and we share it when we evangelize. It is also how we evangelize. Not just through words, but through deeds. Not just through what we say, but through how we live. Not just through what we share with others, but through what we bear for others.

This is our call. This is our mission. This is the New Evangelization.

# NOTES

1. Abby Johnson, *Unplanned* (Carol Stream, IL: Tyndale Momentum, 2011).

2. Interview with Raymond Arroyo, "The World Over" (October 10, 2012).

3. William Doino, "The Long Journey Home," *Inside the Vatican* (January 7, 2008).

4. Pew Research Center's Forum on Religion & Public Life, "U.S. Religious Landscape Survey" (2008).

5. Sherry A. Weddell, *Forming Intentional Disciples: The Path to Knowing and Following Jesus* (Huntington, IN: Our Sunday Visitor, 2012), p. 62.

6. Pope John Paul II, Address to CELAM (Opening Address of the Nineteenth General Assembly of CELAM [March 9, 1983], Port-au-Prince, Haiti), *L'Osservatore Romano*, English Edition 16/780 (April 18, 1983), n. 9.

7. Pope John Paul II, *Redemptoris Missio* (on the permanent validity of the Church's missionary mandate) (Vatican City: Libreria Editrice Vaticana, 1990), n. 86: "The number of those awaiting Christ is still immense: the human and cultural groups not yet reached by the Gospel, or for whom the Church is scarcely present, are so widespread as to require the uniting of all the Church's resources. As

she prepares to celebrate the jubilee of the year 2000, the whole Church is even more committed to a new missionary advent. We must increase our apostolic zeal to pass on to others the light and joy of the faith, and to this high ideal the whole People of God must be educated."

8. George Weigel, "Denver and Toronto: Opportunities Seized, Opportunities Missed," *The Catholic Difference* (July 7, 2003).

9. Pope John Paul II's speech upon his arrival at Denver's Stapleton International Airport (August 12, 1993).

10. Pope Benedict XVI, "Address to the Participants in the International Conference on the 40th anniversary of the Conciliar Decree *Ad Gentes*" (March 11, 2006).

11. Pope Benedict XVI, "Letter to Cardinal Ivan Dias, Prefect of the Congregation for the Evangelization of Peoples, on the Occasion of the Mission Year in Lisieux" (September 12, 2007).

12. Benedict XVI, "Message to the Young People of the World on the Occasion of the 24th World Youth Day" (February 22, 2009).

13. Pope Benedict XVI, "Letter to the Bishops of the Catholic Church Concerning the Remission of the Excommunication of the Four Bishops Consecrated by Archbishop Lefebvre" (March 10, 2009).

14. As quoted in George Weigel's *Evangelical Catholicism: Deep Reform in the 21st-Century Church* (New York: Doubleday, 2013), p. ix.

15. Pope Benedict XVI, *Sacramentum Caritatis* ("The Sacrament of Charity"), n. 46; *Verbum Domini* ("The Word of the Lord"), n. 35.

16. Emily Stimpson, "Evangelization: Ways of Witnessing," *Our Sunday Visitor Newsweekly*, March 21, 2010.

17. Avery Cardinal Dulles, S.J., *Evangelization for the Third Millennium* (Mahwah, NJ: Paulist, 2009).

18. *Lumen Gentium*, n. 11; cf. *Roman Ritual*, Rite of Confirmation, Introduction 2.

19. Francis George, "Catholicity and the New Evangelization," *Catholicity and the New Evangelization: Proceedings from the Seventeenth Convention of the Fellowship of Catholic Scholars*, edited by Anthony J. Mastroeni (Steubenville, OH: Franciscan University Press, 1995), p. 3.

20. Joseph Cardinal Ratzinger, "Address to Catechists and Religion Teachers, at the Jubilee of Catechists" (December 12, 2000).

21. Cyprian, *Ad Donatum*, 3-4.

22. St. Justin Martyr. Adapted from "The First Apology of Justin," *Ante-Nicene Fathers: The Apostolic Fathers, Justin Martyr, Irenaeus* (Vol. 1), translated by Alexander Roberts, James Donaldson, and A. Cleveland Coxe (Buffalo, NY: Christian Literature Publishing Company, 1885), p. 183.

23. Rodney Stark, *The Rise of Christianity* (San Francisco: HarperSanFrancisco, 1997), pp. 97 and 118.

24. Ibid., pp. 97–98.

25. Ibid., p. 106.

26. Ibid., pp. 99–101.

27. Ibid. See pp. 73–94 for Stark's full discussion on mass epidemic and conversion.

28. Ibid., p. 81.

29. Ibid., p. 84.

30. Adapted from "The Epistle of Mathetes to Diognetus," *The Ante-Nicene Fathers*, pp. 25–30.

31. John Paul II, *Puebla: A Pilgrimage of Faith* (Boston: Daughters of St. Paul, 1979), p. 86.

32. Pope Benedict XVI, "Homily for the Opening of the Synod of Bishops and Proclamation of St. John of Ávila and of St. Hildegard of Bingen as Doctors of the Church" (October 7, 2012).

33. St. Augustine, Sermon 94.1.

34. Tertullian, "On Prayer," *The Ante-Nicene Fathers* (Vol. 3), translated by S. Thelwall, pp. 681–691.

35. *Acts of the Abitinian Martyrs*, 10–13 (Migne, PL 8.696–698).

36. Tertullian, *Apology* 39. Quoted in *The Rise of Christianity*, p. 87.

37. For a more detailed (and expert) discussion on cultivating the family in your home and making homes havens of charity, see Kimberly Hahn's four-book series on marriage and family life: *Chosen and Cherished: Biblical Wisdom for Your Marriage* (Cincinnati: St. Anthony Messenger Press, 2007), *Graced and Gifted: Biblical Wisdom for the Homemaker's Heart* (Cincinnati: St. Anthony Messenger Press, 2008), *Beloved and Blessed: Biblical Wisdom for Family Life* (Cincinnati: St. Anthony Messenger Press, 2011), and *Legacy of Love: Biblical Wisdom for Parenting Teens and Young Adults* (Cincinnati: St. Anthony Messenger Press, 2011).

38. *The Rise of Christianity*, p. 6.

39. For more on how single people can understand and respond to God's call to the New Evangelization, see Emily Stimpson's *The Catholic Girl's Survival Guide to the Single Years* (Steubenville, OH: Emmaus Road Publishing, 2012).

40. *Forming Intentional Disciples*. See pages 125-184 for a fuller discussion of the "threshholds" to discipleship.

41. See David Kinnaman's *unChristian: What a New Generation Really Thinks About Christianity … And Why It Matters* (Grand Rapids, MI: Baker Books, 2007), and Christian Smith and Melinda Lundquist Denton's *Soul Searching: The Religious and Spiritual Lives of American Teenagers* (New York: Oxford University Press, 2005).

42. Pope Benedict XVI, "Message for the 47th World Communications Day" (January 24, 2013).

43. In another book, I've talked about Opus Dei and the ways this amazing movement has affected my life as a husband,

father, and teacher. To read more about that, see *Ordinary Work, Extraordinary Grace* (New York: Doubleday, 2006).

44. Pope John Paul II, "Speech, Meeting With Ecclesial Movements and New Communities" (May 30, 1998), n. 7.

45. Council of Trent, Decree on Original Sin (1546).

46. St. Thomas Aquinas, *Summa Theologica* I, Q1, a10, ad 3.

47. Joseph Ratzinger, "Vicarious Representation," translated by Jared Wicks, S.J., in *Letter & Spirit* (Vol. 7) (Steubenville, OH: Emmaus Road, 2011), pp. 209-220.

48. St. Gregory of Nazianzus. Adapted from "Select Letters of Saint Gregory Nazianzen," *A Select Library of the Christian Church: Nicene and Post-Nicene Fathers, Second Series: Cyril of Jerusalem, Gregory Nazianzen* (Vol. 7), edited by P. Schaff and H. Wace, translated by C.G. Browne and J.E. Swallow (New York: Christian Literature Publishing Company, 1894), p. 440. Gregory's famous formula captures well the theology that is already present in the third book of St. Irenaeus' *Against Heresies*.

49. St. Irenaeus of Lyons, "Irenaeus Against Heresies," *The Ante-Nicene Fathers*, p. 424.

50. Carle Zimmerman, *Family and Civilization* (New York: Harper and Brothers, 1947), pp. 120-210.

51. Ibid., pp. 128-129.

52. *Puebla: A Pilgrimage of Faith*, p. 86.

53. Pope Francis, "Sunday Angelus Address" (March 17, 2013).

54. Joseph Cardinal Ratzinger, "Address on the New Evangelization, at the Jubilee of Catechists" (December 12, 2000).

55. Pope Benedict XVI, "General Audience Remarks" (September 17, 2008).

56. Joseph Cardinal Ratzinger, *God Is Near Us: The Eucharist, The Heart of Life* (San Francisco: Ignatius, 2003), p. 40.

57. Peter Kreeft, introduction to *Rome Sweet Home*, by Scott and Kimberly Hahn (San Francisco: Ignatius Press, 1993), p. vii.

58. *God Is Near Us*, p. 37.